Latin
Inscriptions

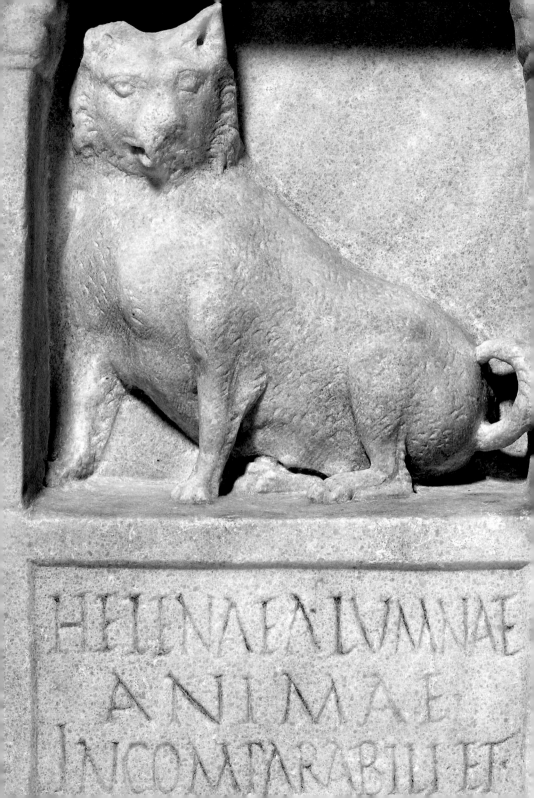

Latin
Inscriptions

Dirk Booms

The J. Paul Getty Museum
Los Angeles

© 2016 The Trustees of the British Museum

Dirk Booms has asserted the right to be identified as the author of this work.

Published in the United States of America by the J. Paul Getty Museum, Los Angeles

Getty Publications
1200 Getty Center Drive, Suite 500
Los Angeles, California 90049-1682
www.getty.edu/publications

Bobby Birchall, Bobby and Co., *Designer*
Kurt Hauser, *Cover Designer*

Distributed in the United States and Canada by the University of Chicago Press

Printed in China

ISBN 978-1-60606-466-5
Library of Congress Control Number: 2015959037

Published simultaneously in the United Kingdom by
The British Museum Press
A division of The British Museum Company Ltd
38 Russell Square, London WC1B 3QQ
britishmuseum.org/publishing

The papers used by The British Museum Press are recyclable products and the manufacturing processes are expected to conform to the environmental regulations of the country of origin.

Frontispiece: Grave stele for Helena (detail, p. 94). Roman, AD 150–200. Los Angeles, J. Paul Getty Museum, 71.AA.271.

Contents

Introduction

Visitors to Roman sites or museums are usually confronted with Latin inscriptions in various shapes and forms. The experience can be confusing. At first sight the letters and abbreviations may reveal little structure or meaning, and the temptation is to look briefly and move on. Yet the truth is that most Latin inscriptions are easy to understand, even with little or no knowledge of the language itself, because they are extremely standardized and formulaic. With minimal effort it is possible to learn the conventions used, and so discover how to read the inscriptions. This becomes more a question of decipherment than of translation: in most cases it is possible to puzzle them out.

The aim of this book is to show not only how you can do this, but also why the effort is so worthwhile. Even the smallest piece of information that an inscription provides can help historians and archaeologists to reconstruct the micro-levels of Roman history. While surviving Latin literature mostly relates to the lives of the emperors and the elite (the people who could afford to read, and indeed to write, books), inscriptions were texts used and seen by all. Thus they shed light on the lives of those classes of people less visible in the archaeological record, such as women, the poor and slaves. Inscriptions reveal aspects of the comradeship of soldiers, of family relations, of the meanings of names, of devastation at the death of a loved one. Some enable us to follow in the footsteps of prominent officials in the complex system of Roman administration and government, and disclose how such men worked their way up from junior bureaucrats to governors of provinces. Others add information to those famous names we already know from literary sources, while the odd one might even let us catch a glimpse into the mind of a stonemason faced with editing out the name of a condemned emperor.

Latin inscriptions follow the rules of Latin grammar, but this book is intended to be usable for a total novice and so guides readers at every step of the way to decipher them. Vocabulary is kept simple, grammatical cases are explained and the rules are rationalized and repeated whenever necessary.

The majority of inscriptions that have come down to us from the Roman world are funerary inscriptions, and this preponderance is reflected in this book. Funerary inscriptions actually form the perfect introduction to the medium, as their brevity and their standardization throughout the Empire meant that almost every Roman, including the illiterate or semi-literate, could understand them. Personal names are naturally an important feature of inscriptions of this type. They need no translation, of course, yet are immediately fascinating: they not only show the typical three-part naming system of the Romans, but also instantly demonstrate the wide variety of nationalities and classes that made up the Empire.

In the following chapters such memorials to the dead play a large part, although they are considered along with other inscription types. Each chapter deals with a particular theme, highlighting the type of information that each group of selected inscriptions provides. The range is wide, from the significance of grand official titles to the expression of deep human emotion. This approach seems important: it is certainly fun to treat inscriptions like word puzzles, and the reader will be encouraged to do just that, but ultimately it is the information released that truly matters, and the insight we can gain into Roman lives, minds and hearts.

CHAPTER ONE

Recording on Stone

To reconstruct the history of the Roman Republic and
Empire, we rely heavily on both archaeological remains
and contemporary literature. Both come with obvious
problems. Material remains of buildings and objects are
plentiful, but entirely subject to accidents of preservation.
We can never be sure that we receive a balanced picture,
and we know that some aspects of Roman life are
scarcely represented. Roman literature is another rich
source of insight and information, but the bias towards
the concerns of the elite writing class has already been
mentioned. Ordinary, everyday events were not
considered worthy of recording, while the lower classes,
if present at all in literary works, were recorded through
an elite interpretation that could descend into caricature.
Inscriptions thus become an immensely important
category of evidence surviving from Roman times which
generally does not present the same difficulties. Both
archaeological and literary, they are found in great
numbers in every Roman city in every corner of the
Empire, from Morocco and Spain to Azerbaijan. As
original documents, most of them contemporary with the
events they record, they are usually less biased than
literary sources (though often the historians who use them
are not). Since the practice of inscribing pervaded every
layer of the population, we can learn about events
pertaining to emperors, local magistrates and slaves alike.
Inscriptions on stone record an enormous range of

information, depending on the type of inscription with which we are dealing. Most of them fall into a handful of categories: funerary inscriptions, on tombstones or commemorative plaques; building inscriptions, commemorating the construction of private and public monuments; dedications, either to individuals (often, but not exclusively on statue bases), to the ruler or to the gods (often on an altar); and many kinds of public documents, including calendars, laws, treaties and decrees. Inscriptions do not just survive on stone, however, although those comprise the majority of the examples considered in this book. Any type of inscribing, be it on a terracotta cup, a roof tile or a bronze figurine, as well as the legend on a coin – a few of which are included in this book – is referred to as an inscription.

The Roman practice of inscribing stone goes back to the beginnings of Roman history. The earliest surviving monumental inscription from Rome itself, dated to the early sixth century BC, is on a stele underneath the so-called 'black stone' pavement in the Roman Forum, the *lapis niger* (fig. 1). The stele was inscribed in an archaic form of Latin, not all of which can be translated. However, since it contains the word *recei* (the archaic dative form of the word *rex*, 'king'), it was immediately linked to the mythical kings of early Rome upon its discovery. Interpretations of the stone vary greatly, especially since the real meaning was already forgotten by the later Republic, when authors thought of it as the 'tomb of Romulus', the first king of Rome, or the base for a statue of the same king. The current, more informed opinion considers the inscription to be a set of laws and regulations linked to the local cult of Vulcan, god of fire and one of the earliest Roman cults.

Overall, inscriptions on stone from the Roman Republican era (traditionally from the expulsion of the kings around 509 BC to the start of Augustus's rule in 27

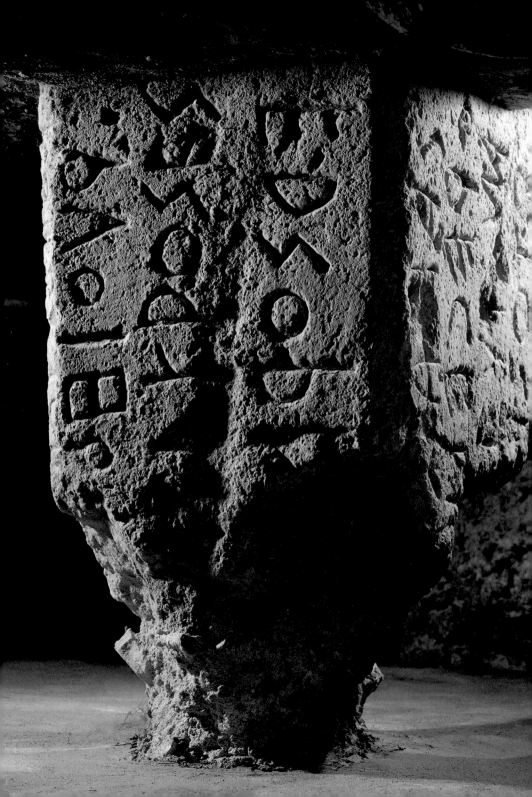

BC) are greatly outnumbered by those surviving from the imperial period (from Augustus until the fall of the Empire, at least in the west, in AD 476). Historians often assume that during the Republic fewer inscriptions were put up, and that the practice increased significantly under the emperors. This must certainly be the case numerically and proportionally, simply because the Empire grew so much larger than before. It is, however, also the unfortunate case that fewer inscriptions from the Republic would have survived until today as they were recorded on less durable stone, such as limestone and tufa. Only in the mid-first century BC did the Romans open up the marble quarries in Carrara, after which inscriptions were frequently carved in marble.

Probably the best known Latin inscription comprises just four letters: SPQR. Walking around Rome today it is still omnipresent, both in ancient examples (see fig. 2) and in modern adoptions of it. The acronym stood for *Senatus Populus-que Romanus*, 'the Senate and the People of Rome'. It proudly proclaimed Roman identity and Roman government, and also embodied the superiority that the Romans felt over other cultures and peoples, hence its dispersal throughout the Empire.

Most inscriptions were intended to record a maximum amount of information in as short a text as possible. Both marble and carving were expensive, and therefore each inscription was the result of careful consideration and a balance between cost and the information that needed to be conveyed. Combined with the highly bureaucratic nature of the Roman world, and the fact that a significant proportion of the population was illiterate or only semi-literate, this resulted in an extremely standardized system for recording information through a fixed number of abbreviations. This allowed people to convey messages through a type of code, highly recognizable even for those unable to read.

Fig. 1 So-called *lapis niger*, Roman Forum, Rome, early 6th century BC.

Fig. 2 OVERLEAF Arch of Constantine, Rome, AD 315. The arch was dedicated by the Senate and the People of Rome (*Senatus Populus-que Romanus*, SPQR) to commemorate Constantine's victory over his co-emperor Maxentius in AD 312.

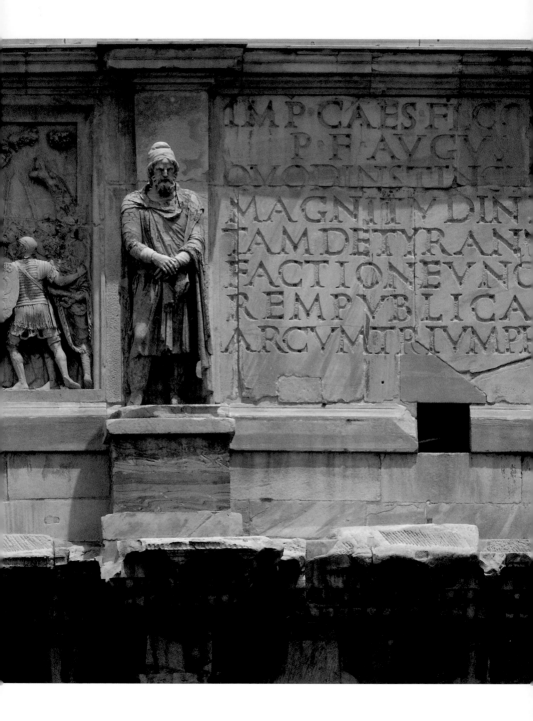

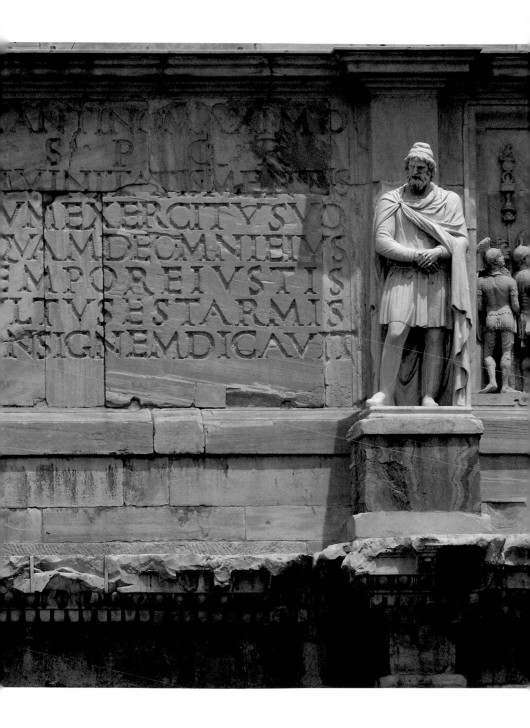

This example – SPQR – neatly demonstrates why there is no actual need to know much Latin in order to understand most inscriptions covered in this book. It does not mean, however, that inscriptions do not follow common rules of spelling and grammar. Even though abbreviated, the texts are often full sentences with subject, object and verb, in their respective grammatical cases.

In very general terms, these are:

- nominative for the subject of the sentence, such as names – Umpricius Aburcus (see inscription 1, p. 20)
- accusative for the object, such as *donum dedit*, 'gave a gift' (see inscription 19, p. 83)
- genitive for a possessive, such as *libertis eorum*, 'their freedmen' (see p. 49)
- dative for the indirect object of the verb (or direct object if related to an act of giving) such as *pater filiabus*, 'a father to his daughters' (see inscription 9, p. 50)
- ablative to express adverbial ideas of separation, location, and of means/description, such as *in fronte pedes …*, *in agro pedes …*, '… feet wide, … feet deep' (see p. 48 and inscription 6, p. 32).

	M sing	F sing	N sing	M pl	F pl	N pl
Nom	-us	-a	-um	-i	-ae	-a
Gen	-i/-is	-ae/-is	-i/-is	-orum	-arum	-orum
Dat	-o/-i	-ae/-i	-o/-i	-is/-ibus	-is/-ibus	-is/-ibus
Acc	-um	-am	-um	-os/-es	-as/-es	-a
Abl	-o/-e	-a	-o/-e	-is/-ibus	-is/-ibus	-is/-ibus

Though this may seem daunting at first, the examples in the book show that it is usually very easy to identify the subject of the text. The reader will learn as he or she goes on, and will find that accompanying explanations become less and less necessary as the abbreviations used are encountered again and again, so that the conventions become familiar.

In the book each inscription is accompanied by a photograph of the object bearing the inscription, a transcription of the text, a transliteration of the text (in which the abbreviations have been completed), a translation and finally an interpretation of the text. The Romans made reading a Latin inscription fairly easy for us because, unlike Greek inscriptions, individual words are almost always separated by dots. In addition we have no problem in reading the Latin script. Capital letters are used, and the only difference the modern English reader will find is that the Romans did not have the letters J, U or W, while K, X and Z occur rarely. Academic conventions in the transliterations of the text are also simple: round brackets are used to indicate the completion of an abbreviation, square brackets and horizontal dashes are used for the reconstruction of missing parts of the text and a forward slash is used to indicate a new line. In the body of the text abbreviations are printed in bold, sometimes with their completion added between brackets. In all, it is hoped that the reader will find the system completely self-explanatory.

CHAPTER TWO

What's in a Name?

The one element that is present in every dedicatory inscription in the Roman world is either the name of the person for whom it was made or the person responsible for setting it up. Whether it was a dedication to the emperor or gods, a commemoration of a building or a tombstone set up for a friend or family member, the name of the person paying for the inscription often took the most important place. Therefore to read, understand and interpret an inscription it is best always to start with the name or names.

The display of a name was important in extremely hierarchical Roman society, since a person's social status, lineage and sometimes even place of origin could all be read in just their name. By the imperial period, slaves had only one name, free women usually two and a free male citizen had three. However, in the early Republic Roman citizens only had two names: a *praenomen* (first name) and a *nomen*. The *nomen*, which we would translate as 'family name', indicated which *gens* (plural: *gentes*) the citizen was a member of. The *gens* was one of the core elements of the Roman social structure; it consisted of all families that had the same *nomen* and claimed descent from a common ancestor. However, as more and more families with the same *nomen* rose to prominence, and given the paucity of original first names (there really were only fifteen common ones and first sons usually took that of the father), a third name, the *cognomen*, became necessary to distinguish between different branches of these families or between individual members. The *cognomen* originally was a nickname, given to a person for any memorable characteristic, be it a personal trait (e.g. Lepidus, 'charming'), a visual trait (e.g. Crassus, 'fat', or Ahenobarbus, 'bronze/red-beard') or a famous deed or victory (e.g. Magnus or 'The Great', for Gnaeus Pompeius, a name awarded for his many victories as general). After a while, however, this *cognomen* became hereditary (e.g. Pompey's son also took on Magnus as *cognomen*).

An inscription relating to a free Roman male will therefore usually display all three names, of which the *praenomen* was almost always abbreviated (see list). The *nomen* was usually written in full, although the *gentes* to which the emperors belonged rose to such prominence and fame that their *nomen* could also be abbreviated. Following *praenomen* and *nomen*, the patriarchal nature of Roman society meant that the abbreviated *praenomen* of the father was also included, in the genitive (not his *nomen*, as that would be identical to that of the son), as well as the word *filius*, 'son', equally in abbreviated form (**F** or **FIL**); together they meant 'son of'. To complete the official name of a free Roman citizen, the *cognomen* was written out in full.

Most common praenomina *of Roman citizens*

A (ulus)	**M** (arcus)	**SER** (vius)
C (aius)	**M** (anius)	**SEX** (tus)
CN (aeus)	**N** (umerius)	**S** (purius) or **Sp**
D (ecimus)	**P** (ublius)	**T** (itus)
L (ucius)	**Q** (uintus)	**TI** (berius)

Abbreviated nomina

AEL (ius)	**CL** (audius)	**IVL** (ius) or **IVLI**
AVR (elius)	**FL** (avius)	**VLP** (ius)

During the later Roman Republic clear examples of this elaborate naming system appear very frequently on coins, as being moneyer for the Roman mint was the first post for a new official. This way a moneyer could literally make a name for himself, as his name was to be seen and read by all who used the newly minted coins. The example illustrated here (fig. 3) was minted by the father of Julius Caesar, moneyer in 103 BC.

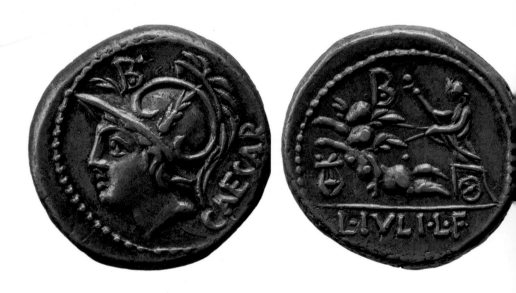

Fig. 3: Silver denarius, minted by Lucius Julius Caesar in 103 BC, showing a helmeted head of Mars, and Venus in a chariot.

The *praenomen* and abbreviated *nomen* **L**(*ucius*) **IVLI**(*us*), as well as the father's *praenomen* Lucius, **L**(*ucii*) **f**(*ilius*), are inscribed on one side of the coin, while the *cognomen* **CAESAR** stands out clearly on the reverse.

Although it appears only rarely in inscriptions, the voting unit or *tribus* to which a citizen belonged followed the patronym. Every free citizen of the entire Roman Empire was officially enrolled in one of thirty-five voting tribes of the city of Rome and, just like the father's name, the *tribus* was an official component of any free individual's name. Therefore more importance was given to them by the upper classes and by new citizens (alien people who received citizenship). The full list is given here for completeness.

Voting tribes

AEM (ilia)

ANI (ensis)

ARN (ensis)

CAM (ilia)

CLA (udia)

CLV (stumina)

COL (lina)

COR (nelia)

ESQ (uilina)

FAB (ia)

FAL (erna)

GAL (eria)

HOR (atia)

LEM (onia)

MAE (cia)/**MAEC**

MEN (enia)

OVF (entina)

PAL (atina)

PAP (iria)

POB (lilia)/**PVB**

POL (lia)

POM (ptina)

PVP (inia)

QVI (rina)

ROM (ilia)

SAB (atina)

SCA (ptia)/**SCAP**

SER (gia)

STE (llatina)/**STEL**

SVB (urana)/**SVC** (cusana)

TER (etina)

TRO (mentina)

VEL (ina)

VOL (tinia)

VOT (uria)

PRICVS C F
BVRCVS Q
OLINEI DAT

1

[- V]MPRICIVS · C · F
ABVRCVS · Q
[AP]OLINEI · DAT

[- U]mpricius C(aii) f(ilius) / Aburcus q(uaestor) /
[Ap]olinei dat

[-] Umpricius Aburcus, son of Gaius, quaestor,
gives (dat) (this) to Apollo (Apolinei)

Umpricius Aburcus are a *nomen* and *cognomen*: the praenomen is missing. Aburcus's name is recorded in the nominative, making him the subject of the action. Caii is the genitive form of Caius, so just the two letters **C F** tell us the name of Umpricius Aburcus's father. The name of the god Apollo is in the dative, making him the one to whom something is dedicated. The dedication was probably a statue and this inscription would have been on its base. A quaestor was one of the magistrates in the Roman system of government (see chapter 4).

Based on the shape of the letters and the archaic type of Latin (with a dative ending in –ei for Apollo), this inscription can be dated to the last decades of the 2nd century BC. Even though it is broken and missing the first letters of two lines, it is of great historic importance: only *c.* 4,300 inscriptions survive from the period from the 6th century BC to the 1st century BC, in contrast to hundreds of thousands from the imperial period. It particularly shows us that the tripartite naming system was already well established by this point, even in an originally non-Roman city. The inscription was found in Falerii. This city was Faliscan in origin (an Italic people in central Italy), but was also one of the earliest cities annexed to Rome to receive citizenship, as early as 386 BC. In fact the archaic form of the name Umbricius with a P might indicate a deliberate recalling of the original Faliscan spelling of the name.

L·COCCEIVS·M·F
DEXEVS
CLYMENVS
VIXIT ANNVM·I
MENSIS·VII
DIEM·VNVM

2

*The upper inscription of two on the same urn
records the deceased's name in the nominative
(the rest of the inscription will be analysed later,
see inscription 8, p. 41).*

L · COCCEIVS · M · F
DEXIVS
CLYMENVS

L(ucius) Cocceius M(arci) f(ilius) / Dexius / Clymenus

Lucius Cocceius Dexius Clymenus, son of Marcus

Once the *cognomen* was fully incorporated as a hereditary family name, it
was not impossible for Romans to receive a fourth name, *agnomen*. Often
these referred to famous deeds, as the *cognomen* had done previously; perhaps
the most famous of all is Africanus, 'of Africa', for Scipio following
his defeat of Hannibal at Zama in North Africa. Sometimes, however, they
could be affectionate nicknames, as on this funerary chest of the little boy
Lucius Cocceius Dexius Clymenus. In mythology, Clymenus, or Klymenos
in Greek, was a son of the sun god Helios.

Slaves had only one name. Sometimes this was a
Latinized form of an originally foreign name, otherwise it
was an entirely newly acquired name – on occasion with
extra connotation or misplaced humour, a practice that can
be found among slave-owners of every era. Slaves had very
few means of their own, yet several thousand inscriptions
commemorating them survive. Most of the time their status
is indicated by the fact they only note one name, but

sometimes it was more explicitly made clear by adding
SER(*vus/a* [m/f]) for 'slave' or **VERNA/VERN**(*a* [same ending
for m/f]) for 'houseborn slave' (a slave born in captivity).
However, slaves could be freed by their masters, a practice
extremely common in Roman society, after which they became
free citizens. If they made a fortune themselves, in the eyes of
the old and aristocratic elite they were perceived as, and treated
similarly to, the *nouveaux riches* of the nineteenth and early
twentieth centuries, an example being the tawdry millionaire
freedman Trimalchio, the protagonist in Petronius's *Satyricon*.

As new citizens, these so-called freedmen needed three
names, so they took on the *praenomen* and *nomen* of their male or
female master, while their own name became the new *cognomen*.
In the official nomenclature, their master's name took the place
of the patronym (a freed slave's actual father was most likely a
slave himself, and so not considered important), followed by
libertus, 'freedman' (abbreviated as **L** or **LIB**), instead of *filius*.
Female slaves, like male ones, had only one name. When freed
they took on two names: just like freedmen, they took the *nomen*
of their master, while their original name became the *cognomen*.

There was a strict hierarchy among slaves, based not only
upon the tasks they had to perform, but also on the status of
their masters. Slaves of the emperor or of the imperial
household enjoyed certain prestige, both while slaves and after
being freed – at which point they were called *Augusti libertus/a*,
'freedman/woman of the emperor' (*libertus*, the subject, in the
nominative and *Augusti* in the genitive case). Such freedmen and
-women often tended to point out their imperial status in
inscriptions. When freed they assumed their master's, i.e. the
emperor's, *praenomen* and *nomen*.

Roman women usually had two names, as noted above.
Neither of them was very original: they were named by the
female form of their father's *nomen* – e.g. Julia for the daughter
of (Gaius) Julius Caesar, or Flavia for the daughter of the
emperor Vespasian (Titus Flavius Vespasianus) – sometimes with
the addition of the father's *cognomen*. Because of the confusion

this naturally generated in an over-populated Rome, women were often given a nickname or second name for identification. Thus Nero's grandmother, officially called Vipsania Agrippa after her father Marcus Vipsanius Agrippa, was known to everyone by the diminutive Agrippina.

A woman could also receive a third name after marriage, written in the genitive case, as from that moment on she transferred from the authority of her father to the authority of her husband. An example of this can be seen in the inscription on the enormous tomb of Caecilia Metella, sited on the Via Appia Antica outside Rome (fig. 4). She was the daughter of Quintus Caecilius Metellus ('Creticus', after his conquest of Crete), and became Caecilia Metella Crassi after her marriage to Marcus Licinius Crassus. A husband owned his wife's dowry, her inheritance rights and any property acquired during marriage. This extremely unequal custom became less popular towards the end of the Republic, and women were given the possibility of marrying with greater independence and owning property. We recognize this in inscriptions, as from the imperial period onwards we rarely find the name of the husband as part of a woman's name.

Fig. 4: Print by Giovanni Batista Piranesi (*Roman Antiquities*), showing the tomb of Caecilia Metella on the Via Appia Antica outside Rome and the detail of its inscription.

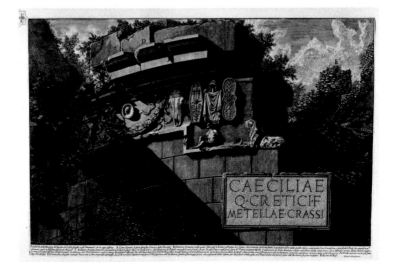

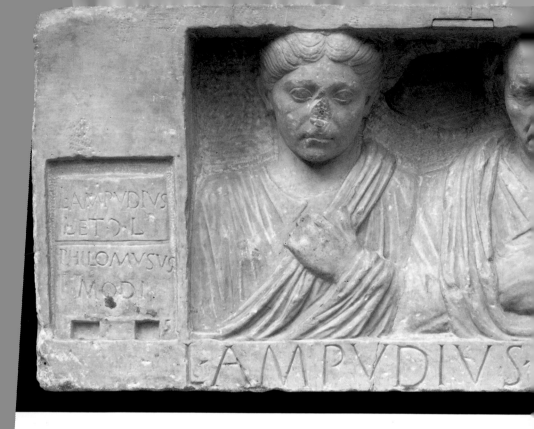

3

L · AMPVDIVS · L · ET · Ɔ · L · PHILOMVSVS

L(ucius) Ampudius L(ucii) et Ɔ (Caiae) l(ibertus) Philomusus

Lucius Ampudius Philomusus, freedman of Lucius and his wife

Through these three complete words, four abbreviations and the depictions on the tombstone, we can reconstruct several aspects of the life of this freedman and his family. We know that his slave name was Philomusus – a

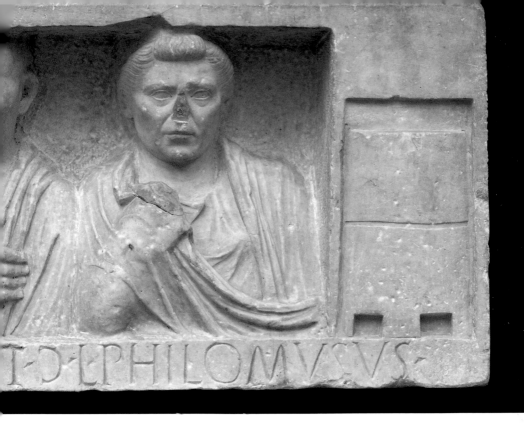

Greek name, which probably indicates that he himself was Greek – and that his master was named Lucius Ampudius, though we do not know his *cognomen*. However, two masters are mentioned on this tombstone: Lucius, as well as his wife, whose name we do not know. To refer to a female master, an inverted C (Ɔ) was used in inscriptions, meaning generically Gaia, 'a woman'.

From the depiction on this so-called freedmen relief, we can date the monument to the early Empire. While Philomusus himself sports a hairstyle and severe facial features that were popular during the later Republic, the hairstyles of his wife and of who is likely their daughter copy those popular at the imperial court of the time, especially that of Livia, wife of the emperor Augustus. Augustus had passed new laws giving more rights to freed slaves, including the right to marry freeborn citizens.

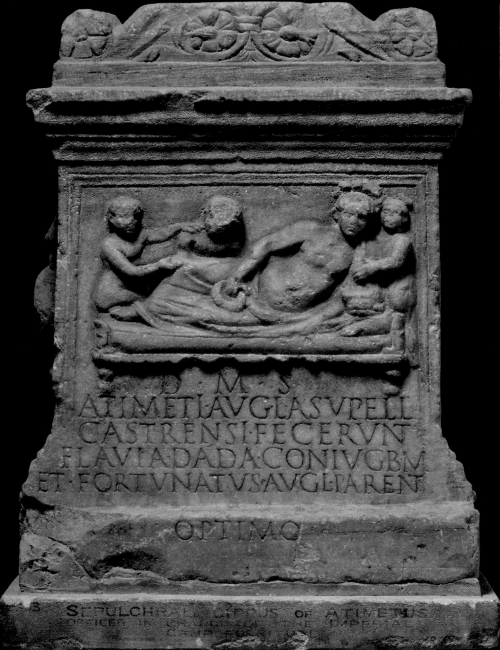

D · M · S
ATIMETIAVGLASVPELL
CASTRENSIFECERVNT
FLAVIADADA·CONIVGBM
ET·FORTVNATVSAVGLPARENT

OPTIMO

4

This small funerary altar was dedicated to
Atimetus by his wife and son.

D · M · S
ATIMETI · AVG · L · A SVPELL
CASTRENSI · FECERVNT
FLAVIA · DADA · CONIVG · B · M
ET · FORTVNATVS · AVG · L · PARENT
OPTIMO

D(is) M(anibus) s(acrum) / Atimeti Aug(usti) l(iberti) a supell(ectile) / castrensi
fecerunt / Flavia Dada coniug(i) b(ene) m(erenti) / et Fortunatus Aug(usti)
l(ibertus) parent(i) / optimo

Sacred to the spirits of the dead and of Atimetus, imperial freedman, keeper of
the furniture of the imperial palace. Flavia Dada dedicated (fecerunt) this to a
well-deserving husband (coniugi, dative of coniunx), and Fortunatus, imperial
freedman, to the best of parents (parenti optimo, dative of parens optimus).

Space probably did not permit Atimetus and his son Fortunatus to display
their full names. However, given the *nomen* Flavia of Dada, Atimetus's wife
and a fellow freed slave, it is more than likely that their *nomen* was Flavius
as well, and that all three had been freed by one of the Flavian emperors
(AD 69–96) or their family members.

Atimetus had quite an important task at the imperial palace (sometimes
called *castrum*, military camp), as he was responsible for the upkeep of all
furniture. The inscription is a fine example of the bi-partite name of a female
freedwoman, and potentially of the 'ironic' nature of many slave names. More
common than any other slave names were Fortunatus, 'Lucky', Felix, 'Happy'
or, in Greek, Soteria, 'Salvation'. In this case, however, his own parents may
have named him so, as he truly was luckier than some to be born into the
imperial household.

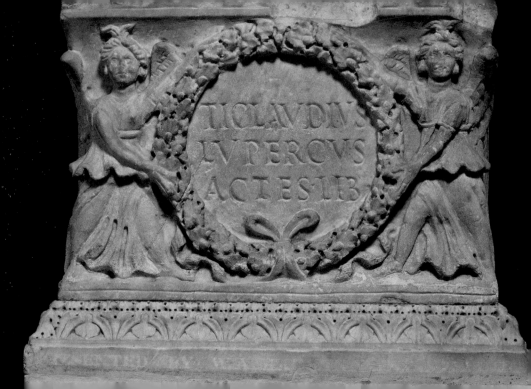

5

*Freedmen and -women could, and often did, own
slaves themselves, as well as free them. This small
funerary chest reads:*

**TI CLAVDIVS
LVPERCVS
ACTES · LIB**

Ti(berius) Claudius / Lupercus / Actes lib(ertus)

Tiberius Claudius Lupercus, freedman of Acte

This is one of those instances in which an inscription can be linked
to a historical figure. Through Lupercus's full name, we can deduce
that his mistress was called Claudia Acte. Without a doubt she is
the freedwoman who became mistress and influential advisor
to the emperor Nero, as described in many literary sources
(Suetonius, *Nero* 28 and 50; Dio 61.7.1; Tacitus, *Annals*
13.12–14.2). She herself acquired properties and many
household staff, of whom Lupercus was one before being freed.
He was thus the freedman of a freedwoman.

N · DECVMIVS · N · F
COL · VAARVS · SCR ·
VOLVSIA · C · L · CELSA
C · VOLVSIVS · C · L · CHARIT
IN · F · P · XIII · IN · AGR · LXVI

6

This funerary inscription combines several different examples of Roman nomenclature. It would have been attached to the outside of a monumental tomb. The inscription names three individuals in the nominative, which implies that they took care of the arrangements for their tomb themselves.

**N · DECVMIVS · N · F
COL · VAARVS · SCR ·
VOLVSIA · C · L · CELSA
C · VOLVSIVS · C · L · CHARIT
IN · FR · P · XIII · IN · AGR · P · XVI**

N(umerius) Decumius N(umerii) f(ilius) / Col(lina) Vaarus scr(iba) / Volusia C(aii) l(iberta) Celsa / C(aius) Volusius C(aii) l(ibertus) Charit(es) / in fr(onte) p(edes) XIII in agr(o) p(edes) XVI

Numerius Decumius Vaarus, son of Numerius, of the Collina voting tribe, scribe; Volusia Celsa, freedwoman of Gaius; and Gaius Volusius Charites, freedman of Gaius. (This plot of land is) 13 feet wide and 16 feet deep.

It is clear that the tomb contains the bodies of one freeborn citizen, who makes a point of mentioning his voting tribe, and of two slaves freed by the same master, but the relationship between them remains unclear from this text. One possibility is that Volusia was the wife of Vaarus, although such a 'detail' would usually not be omitted. The last line will be discussed in chapter 3 (see p. 48).

CHAPTER THREE

In Memoriam

As the previous chapter makes clear, a very substantial portion of all Latin inscriptions to survive today are funerary inscriptions. These occur not just on tombstones, but also on epitaph plaques, burial chests, sarcophagi, etc. A tomb of any kind was obviously a costly thing, and we have to assume that not everyone was able to pay for burial, its recording on stone or both. Yet, apart from the extremely poor Romans, who are completely invisible in texts or material culture, we find every layer of society represented in the body of funerary inscriptions, indicating the enormous importance given to a lasting legacy, if only through a small tombstone.

It is no coincidence that the Latin word *monumentum* was frequently used for 'tomb'. After the emergence of the emperors, the wealthy aristocratic families were left unable to promote themselves in public, so producing a visible, grand and lavish tomb was one of the few ways in which they could still compete with each other and remain prominent in city life. Yet Roman law forbade anyone to be buried within the sacred city boundaries and so tombs usually lined the main access roads to cities. Grander and more prominent tombs were closest to the city, with smaller ones set further out. The remnants of those grandiose monuments of the Roman aristocracy still line the Via Appia outside Rome.

We have already seen the example of the freedmen,

whose main concern was to record their free status for posterity. However, many funerary inscriptions convey a much wider variety of information, as obviously different people or groups of people were concerned with recording different kinds of information and facts. In this chapter we will first look at some elements found in inscriptions of any type, after which we focus on two different classes of funerary inscriptions.

Names, as seen above, were the most important element of a funerary inscription. The simplest form of inscription consists of just one name, that of the deceased, in the nominative case. However, many inscriptions also mention the name of the person who made or dedicated the tomb to the deceased, whether that was a family member, a friend or a colleague, and whether or not this was because of a legal obligation to do so as heir or undertaken through friendship, loyalty, gratitude or any other type of emotional bond. Roman society being obsessed with self-promotion, however, the dedicant's name is sometimes placed in a more prominent position, at the beginning or at the end of the text, and in the nominative case. The name of the deceased then takes the dative case, as the tomb was dedicated *to* the deceased.

Funerary inscriptions are packed with standard abbreviations. The deceased was often **BENE MERENTI**, 'well deserving' (also abbreviated as **B M**, **BENE MER** or any other variant). In the case of a dedication by another, the different cases for the names made it clear who was the dedicant, but still the words **FEC**(*it*) or **FEC**(*erunt*), 'made this', could be added (as in Atimetus's inscription). These were sometimes abbreviated to just **F** (not to be confused with F for *filius*, which is always placed within someone's name).

Alternatively one could write **POS**(*uit*) or **POS**(*uerunt*), 'placed', **DED**(*icavit*) or **DED**(*icaverunt*), 'dedicated', or **F C** or **FAC CVR**, *faciendum curavit/curaverunt*, 'made sure that (it) was made'. Of importance was the addition of **D S** = **(DE) SVO** or **DE S**(*ua*) **P**(*ecunia*), each translating as 'with his/her own money'; they conveyed the dedicant's generous nature as well as his or her financial means.

The second most important element was the deceased's age at death. Unlike our practice today, Romans did not record the year of their death; it was much more important for them to record how long someone had lived. In inscriptions the time that the deceased had lived is indicated by the words *annos*, *annorum* or *annis* (the plural accusative, genitive and ablative declensions of *annus*, 'year'), followed by the number in Roman numerals. Often they are abbreviated to **AN** or **ANN**. The accusative and ablative (the latter by far the most frequently used case) could be preceded by *vixit*, 'he/she lived', or by its abbreviation **VIX** (also **QVI VIX**, 'who lived'). The different declensions mean slightly different things, which can be conveyed through different English translations. *Annos* is an accusative of time, '(lived) x years' (accusative used for time on the Clymenus inscription, inscription 8, p. 40); *annorum* is a genitive of quality, '(a person) x years (old)' (see Marcus Cocceius Nonnus, inscription 25, p. 102); *annis* is an ablative of time within which something happened, '(lived) for x years' (all the other examples in the book).

Around the late first century AD people started recording more than just the number of years they had lived. In a society that believed strongly in the afterlife it was important to know not only the number of years of a person's life, but also the months and days; in some cases even the hour of the day on which the person had died was recorded. Like *annus* they could be put in either of the same three declensions, and were often, but not always, abbreviated as **M**(*enses* (or *mensis*)/*ensium*/*ibus*)), from *mensis*, 'month', **D**(*ies*/*ierum*/*iebus*), from *dies*, 'day' and **H**(*oras*/*orarum*/*oris*), from *hora*, 'hour'. Historians have traditionally interpreted the recording of someone's age to within that last detail as an indication of affection or education, especially since it is recorded for people of all ages and social classes. However, new studies show that the hour was used for astrological calculations, to see which deity was in which position in the firmament – and thus which god would be the protector of the deceased in the afterlife.

In the early first century AD a new expression entered the corpus of funerary formulae: **DIS MANIBVS (SACRVM)**, or abbreviated to **D M (S)**. From then on this expression was used with almost no exception as the first line, making it also the most easily recognizable. In Roman religion the *Di Manes*, or just *Manes*, were protective deities linked to the spirits/souls of the deceased. The formula, in the dative case, therefore does not refer specifically to the soul of the deceased, but rather dedicates the tomb *to the gods* safeguarding that soul.

There are small subtleties in how the phrase is used. If it is followed by the name of the deceased in the nominative case, one can consider it purely introductory. However, if the dead person's name is in the genitive case the tomb is dedicated to the protective *Di Manes* of said person, as in the tombstone of Atimetus (inscription 4, p. 28) and of Marcus Cocceius Nonnus (inscription 25, p. 102). If the name of the deceased follows in the dative case, the case of Dis Manibus itself, the tomb is dedicated to the Di Manes, as well as to the deceased. Many different translations for *Dis Manibus (sacrum)* are used, but the most common one is still '(Sacred) to the Spirits of the Dead'.

D · M · S ·

FABIOSVPERA
I
TOQVIVXSITAN

NIS · LXXX ·

H·S·E·S·T·T·L

7

D · M · S ·
FABIO SVPERA
TO QVI V^{I}XSIT · AN
NIS ·   L · X · X · X ·
H · S · E · S · T · T · L ·

D(is) M(anibus) s(acrum) / Fabio Supera/to qui vixsit an/nis LXXX / h(ic) s(itus) e(st) s(it) t(ibi) t(erra) l(evis)

Sacred to the Spirits of the Dead. To Fabius Superatus, who lived for 80 years. He lies here, may the earth rest lightly on you.

This inscription shows some of the different elements discussed in this chapter. It was found in a cemetery in Italica, Spain, indicating that the same conventions in vogue for epitaphs in Rome and Italy easily spread to the provinces (yet not without problems: for spelling mistakes see chapter 6).

The final line is a combination of two other existing formulae:
H S E = *hic situs/sita est*, 'he/she lies here' (lit.: 'here is placed'), which was often used at the start of the inscription, and more prominent in the period 1st century BC to 1st century AD.
S T T L = *sit terra tibi levis*, 'may the earth rest lightly on you', which was normally used at the end of the inscription; also when combined with the formula above. The line should be seen as a request for this prayer by the deceased to anyone passing the tomb and reading the epitaph, or represents the words spoken by the passerby to the deceased.

It is of interest that this combination of the two formulae is almost exclusively found in the Spanish provinces, just as the name Superatus or Superata is unattested anywhere but Spain and the North African province of Numidia. Clearly local customs developed over time, even if they are not necessarily linked by familial connections.

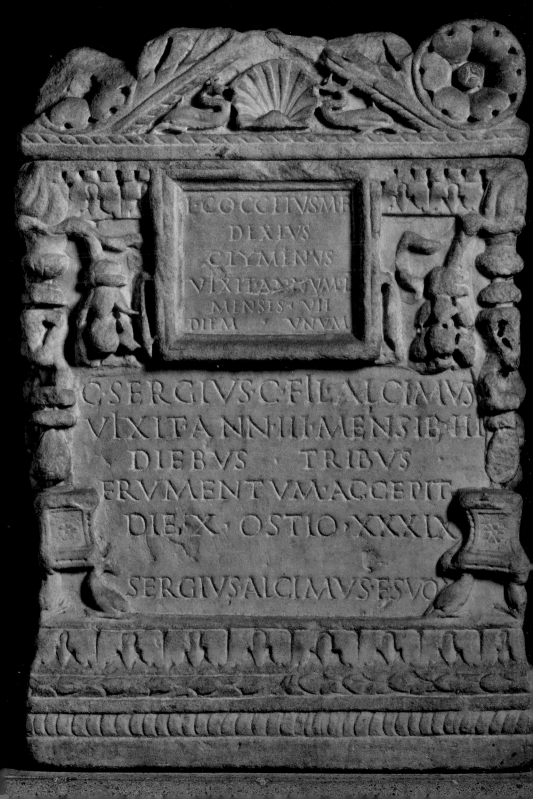

L·COCCEIVS·M·F
DEXIVS
CLYMENVS
VIXIT·ANNVM·I
MENSIS·VII
DIEM·VNVM

C·SERGIVS·C·FIL·ALCIMVS
VIXIT·ANN·III·MENSIB·IIII
DIEBVS·TRIBVS
FRVMENTVM·ACCEPIT
DIE·X·OSTIO·XXXIX

SERGIVS·ALCIMVS·F·SVO

8

L · COCCEIVS · M · F
DEXIVS
CLYMENVS
VIXIT · ANNVM · I
MENSIS · VII
DIEM · VNVM

C · SERGIVS · C · FIL · ALCIMVS
VIXIT · ANN · III · MENSIB · III
DIEBVS · TRIBVS ·
FRVMENTVM · ACCEPIT
DIE · X · OSTIO · XXXIX
SERGIVS · ALCIMVS · F · SVO

a) L(ucius) Cocceius M(arci) f(ilius) / Dexius / Clymenus / vixit annum I /
mensis VII / diem unum
b) C(aius) Sergius C(aii) fil(ius) Alcimus / vixit ann(is) III mensib(us) III /
diebus tribus / frumentum accepit / die X ostio XXXIX / Sergius Alcimus
f(ecit) (de) suo

a) Lucius Cocceius Dexius Clymenus, son of Marcus, lived 1 year,
7 months and 1 day.
b) Gaius Sergius Alcimus, son of Gaius, lived for 3 years, 3 months and 3 days.
He received (accepit) the grain dole (frumentum) on the 10th day at Gate 39.
Sergius Alcimus made (this tomb) with his own money.

This burial chest contained the ashes of two children, whose names do not
reveal a familial relationship. Re-use of sarcophagi and burial chests was a
fairly common occurrence in the Roman Empire, and often happened
illegally by simply placing remains in an already occupied vessel. In this case,
however, the fact that any previous decoration was carefully erased from the
front surface of the chest to make room for the second inscription, a laborious
task – or was even planned to hold it from the beginning – makes it more

likely that there must have been a connection, now untraceable, between the families of the boys.

By now the formulae will be easily understood by the reader. However, the reconstruction of the final line is not completely certain. Apart from the version above, another possibility is *Sergius Alcimus f(ilio) suo*, 'Sergius Alcimus (dedicates this) to his son'. This shows that with such a mass of abbreviations in inscriptions, duplications tend to emerge.

Of further interest, however, is the line *frumentum accepit die X ostio XXXIX*. It was important for the father of the child, the Sergius Alcimus mentioned in the last line, to point out that his son had received the grain dole, indicating he had been a free citizen. Does this mean that the father was a freedman? Possibly, even though the inscription does not say it. From the mid-1st century AD onwards freedmen increasingly omitted their status. Because of the enormous undertaking that handing out the grain dole to free citizens was (during most of the Principate 200,000 citizens of Rome received a monthly dole), people were assigned a specific day of the month (here the 10th) and a specific gate (here the 39th, of 45 in total) at the Porticus Minucia Frumentaria, a large warehouse next to the modern Largo Argentina in Rome.

Fig. 5 Model of ancient Rome, made by the archaeologist Italo Gismondi between 1935 and 1971. In the top centre of the image, the Porticus Minucia Frumentaria is visible next to the four temples of the Largo Argentina (top left).

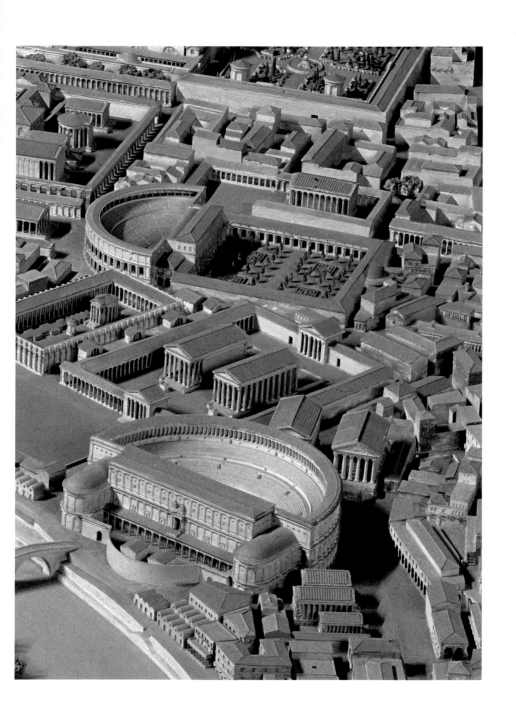

Columbaria

The following Latin inscriptions take the form of small rectangular epitaph plaques. Some contain nothing more than a name, but others also record the age of the deceased. Such standardized plaques would have been set into a wall by a niche that contained the terracotta funerary urn with the deceased's ashes. Urns containing the remains of people of both the lower and middle classes were set, sometimes hundreds of them together, in underground chambers called *columbaria* (singular: *columbarium*). The plaques frequently have decorations, specifically the triangular 'handles' on the side in imitation of the actual handles on bronze plaques, *tabulae ansatae*, which the Romans used for any type of notice to be distributed.

Close to a hundred of the plaques in the British Museum collection come from the same *columbarium* in

Fig. 6 Artist's impression of a generic Roman *columbarium*.

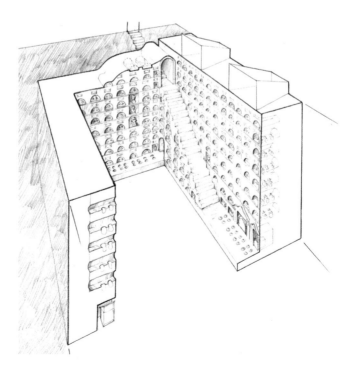

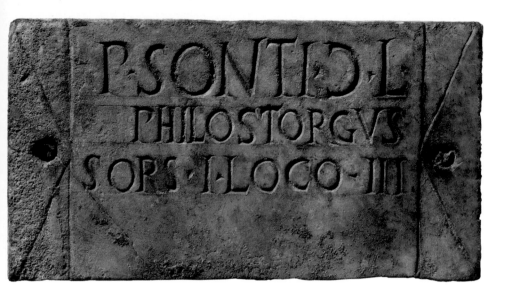

Fig. 7 Ownership
plaque of Publius
Sontius Philostorgus,
from the *columbarium*
'of the thirty-six
partners'.

Rome. It was excavated by one of Rome's early
antiquarians, Francesco Ficoroni, at the beginning of the
eighteenth century, after which the remains were destroyed.
All we know today is that it must have stood near the Porta
Latina, close to the Baths of Caracalla and the starts of
both the Via Latina and Via Appia, two roads along which
many tombs and *columbaria* were erected.

Columbaria were almost exclusively privately owned.
Some belonged to extensive and rich patrician families, in
which their slaves and freedmen could be buried. Others
were owned by guilds (*collegia*) or other organizations to
which one could pay a fee in order to be buried in their
columbarium, while a number were divided up by owners.
The plaque in fig. 7 (above) does not show the name of the
deceased, but instead was a temporary plaque to record the
name of the owner of this particular burial niche, P(ublius)
Sontius Philostorgus, himself a freedman of a female owner
(Ɔ L) Publius owned the third niche (**LOCO III**) on the
bottom row (**SORS I**, counting from bottom to top). This

Fig. 8 Epitaph plaque
for Lucius Scribonius
Zinnaeus, from the
columbarium 'of the
thirty-six partners'.

Fig. 9 Epitaph plaque
for Marcus Titus
Phileros and Flavia
Auge, from the
columbarium 'of the
thirty-six partners'.

columbarium that it comes from, which historians have called 'of the thirty-six partners' (given that we have the names of all thirty-six co-owners), had five rows of niches; each partner seems to have owned one niche on each row to ensure a fair distribution of the most visible niches. The inscriptions recording Philostorgus's niches on the other rows are also known, but went to other European collections.

From the names on these plaques we learn that most of the people buried in this particular *columbarium* were freed slaves, without any other apparent connection. They show

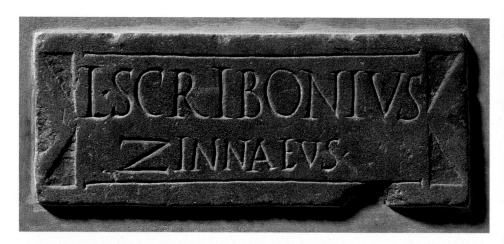

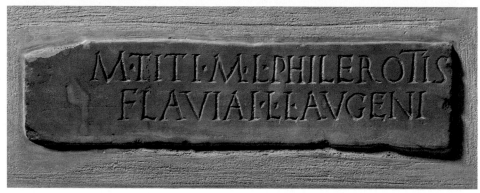

that not all freedmen did as well for themselves as those we know from the literary sources, or find on the so-called freedmen reliefs mentioned above (see inscription 3, p. 26). We also find slaves recorded on the plaques, identifiable by their single name.

Some examples of epitaph plaques of freed slaves from this *columbarium* are illustrated here (figs 8–11), some with *tabula ansata* decoration. On the plaque for L(ucius) Pulfennius Phileros (fig. 10), **L · PVLFENNIVS · L · L · PHILEROS · SCR · LIB**, since the **L · L** already records he was a *libertus*, the additional **LIB** means something else:

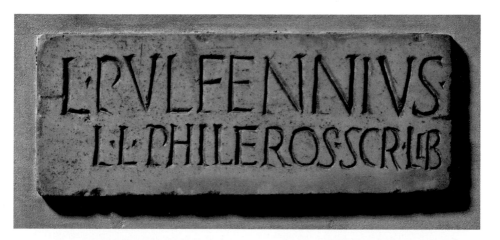

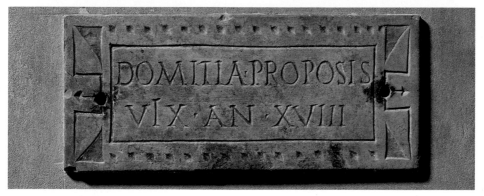

he was a *scriba librarius*, a magistrate's secretary or scribe
(*scriba*; *librarius*, from *liber*: book), which was certainly a
prestigious post. Another plaque (fig. 9) records that
Marcus Titus Phileros, freedman of Marcus, and Flavia
Auge, freedwoman of Lucius, were buried together; and
another (fig. 11) that Domitia Proposis lived for eighteen
years: **VIX · AN · XVIII.**

Monumental tombs

The freestanding tombs of the more wealthy members
of society were obviously of a grander nature than the
underground *columbaria*, even though there was no
blueprint for such tombs and they took a wide variety
of shapes. They were sometimes modelled on, and used,
features of domestic architecture or of other great
monuments, such as the Egyptian pyramids or Greek
mausolea. Inscriptions on monuments of this type
obviously needed to be bigger in order to be visible,
and contained much more information. The so-called
freedmen reliefs are good examples of these inscriptions,
although they focused more on the portrait busts than
on the text itself.

Inscription 6 (p. 32) to Numerius Decumius Vaarus,
apart from being a good example of the different
name-systems one can encounter, also has, as its last line,
a common abbreviation used for tombs: **IN F(R) P ...
IN A(GR) P ....** It describes the exact size of the plot of
land on which the tomb is situated, in Roman feet (which
are almost identical to the modern international
measurement unit of a foot: *c*. 296 to *c*. 305 mm): *in fronte
pedes XIII, in agro pedes XVI*, or '13 feet at the front (i.e.
along the road, hence 'wide'), 16 feet in the field' (i.e.
away from the road, hence 'deep'). Many inscriptions
contain this phrase, or alternatively use **LON**(*gum*) **P ...
LAT**(*um*) **P ...** , 'x feet long, y feet wide'. To record this

information might seem a little strange to us today. In Roman times, however, spelling out legal matters was of extreme importance. Inscribing its size on a tomb itself made sure that the extent of one's land could never be disputed, and descendants could always point this out in case someone contested it or tried to encroach on it.

We have already talked about illegal re-use of tombs and sarcophagi (see Alcimus's chest, inscription 8, p. 40). In an attempt to discourage potential offenders, and also again to show one's duty and obligation, the formula **SIBI ET SVIS** is often repeated; it is sometimes continued with **LIBERTIS LIBERTABVSQVE** and/or **POSTERISQVE EORVM**, or rarely abbreviated to **S E S L L P Q E** or other abbreviated version, for example **S S P E** (*sibi et suis posterisque eorum*). Translated this reads '(made) for him/herself (*sibi*) and family (*suis*; lit. 'his' or 'her'), and (*–que*) to his/her freedmen (*libertis*) and (*–que*) freedwomen (*libertabus)* and (*–que*) their descendants (*posteris eorum*)'. However, an equally commonly used phrase was *hoc monumentum heredem non sequitur*, or **H M H N S,** meaning 'this tomb does not pass to my heir' – making sure that descendants would not sell the land, and the deceased could enjoy the afterlife in peace.

9

***

T · FLAVIVS · AVG · L · ACRABA
DECVRIO · OSTIARIORVM
FECIT · SIBI · ET
HADRIAE · ACRABILLAE
VIX · ANN · VII · MENS · VIIII · D · XVII · H · X · ET
PROVINCIAE · VIXIT
ANNIS · XVIIII
PATER · FILIABVS · BENE · MERENTIBVS · ET
LIBERTIS · LIBERTABVSQ · POSTERISQ · EORVM
IN · FR · P · X · IN · AGR · P · VIIII

T(itus) Flavius Aug(usti) l(ibertus) Acraba / decurio ostiariorum / fecit sibi et / Hadriae Acrabillae / vix(it) ann(is) VII mens(ibus) VIIII d(iebus) XVII h(oris) X et / Provinciae vixit / annis XVIIII / pater filiabus bene merentibus et / libertis libertabusq(ue) posterisq(ue) eorum / in fr(onte) p(edes) X in ag(ro) p(edes) VIIII

Titus Flavius Acraba, imperial freedman and overseer of the doormen, made (this) for himself and for Hadria Acrabilla, who lived for 7 years, 9 months, 17 days, 10 hours, and for Provincia, who lived for 19 years – he was father to well-deserving daughters – and for his freedmen and freedwomen and their descendants. (The tomb is) 10 feet wide and 9 feet deep.

Just like Atimetus (inscription 4, p. 28), Acraba was a freed imperial slave with an important job at the palace, as head of all the porters. With this inscription, he points out that he made this tomb for himself and for all the other members of his family, which included his freedmen and -women. He specifically mentions his two 'well-deserving' daughters, Hadria Acrabilla and Provincia, and the inscription clearly expresses the deeper loss the family must have felt over the death of the young Hadria through the detailed recording of her age at death and her nickname 'little Acraba'.

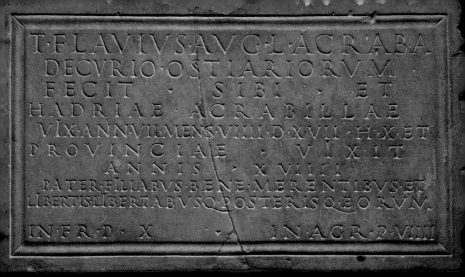

T · FLAVIVS · AVG · L · ACRABA
DECVRIO · OSTIARIORVM ·
FECIT · SIBI · ET
HADRIAE · ACRABILLAE
VIX · ANN · VII · MENS · VIIII · D · XVII · H · X · ET
PROVINCIAE · VIXIT
ANNIS · XVIIII
PATER · FILIABVS · BENE · MERENTIBVS · ET
LIBERTIS · LIBERTABVSQ · POSTERISQ · EORVM
IN · FR · P · X · IN · AGR · P · VIII

Acraba was likely of Jewish origin, as the name is Semitic, which makes the naming of his other daughter 'Province' appear slightly tongue-in-cheek. As his nomen became Flavius upon being freed, it is tempting but not necessarily correct to link his enslavement to the sack of Jerusalem by the emperor Vespasian and his son Titus in AD 71, after which they are said to have transported thousands of Jewish slaves to Rome.

CHAPTER FOUR

Governing an Empire

One particular idiom frequently found in inscriptions, even though very variable in form, is immediately recognizable: the names and titles of the emperor. These titles could be placed on anything relating to the emperor, ranging from grand buildings built by himself or dedicated to him, to statue bases or even coins; they were also used to record dates accurately. The different titles might look familiar to the modern reader, but what do they all mean?

Official lists of titles were completely standardized and, while not all elements were included every time, their sequence became fixed. First one reads **IMP**, for *imperator* – originally a title awarded upon a victory to a commander in the field, but officially made *praenomen* of Julius Caesar by the Senate. The young Octavian (later Augustus) adopted it as *praenomen* from Caesar, his adoptive father. However, the title then all but disappeared from the emperor's official names until Vespasian, who modelled his newly established Flavian dynasty after Augustus, and began to use it as a regular title, meaning 'emperor'. Its place at the head of the titles of every emperor from then onwards signified its importance and the continuing military control the

emperor held. Next is **CAES(AR)**, the *cognomen* of Julius
Caesar that became hereditary to the Julio-Claudian
emperors and was adopted as a title by all emperors
afterwards. Then comes the name of the ruling emperor,
either in full or just the *cognomen*, followed by the title
AVG(VSTVS). This originally meant 'majestic', but after
being awarded to Octavian it passed on to every successive
emperor. Sometimes titles awarded after specific victories
were also included: e.g. Domitian took the title
GERM(*anicus*) for his victory over the Chatti, a Germanic
tribe, while Trajan was awarded the titles *Germanicus* in
AD 97, **DAC**(*icus*) in AD 102 after victory over the
Dacians and **PARTH**(*icus*) in AD 114 after his victory over
the Parthians – a feat that brought the Roman Empire to
its greatest extent.

The emperor also held several prominent magisterial
posts in the government. He was the *pontifex maximus* (**P M,
P MAX** or **PONT MAX**), the chief priest of the Roman
Empire, a title still carried by the Pope today. He had the
tribunicia potestas, the power of a tribune (as *tribunus plebis*,
'tribune of the people': **TR P**, or **TRIB POT**), one of the
oldest offices in Rome and originally instated to protect
the lower classes of people. The title *imperator* (**IMP**) might
be repeated to include the actual number of military
victories the emperor had had. Following this would come
the number of times that the emperor had acted as consul
(**COS**). The two chief magistrates of the Republic were
consuls, an office that continued as a mainly ceremonial
post during the Empire, with the emperor himself voted as
one of the consuls most years. Only sometimes was the
position of censor (**CEN** or **CENSOR**), the magistrate
regulating the census and public morality, recorded,
though every emperor took it up. Almost every emperor,
however, recorded *pater patriae* (**P P** or **PAT PAT**), 'father
of the fatherland', the term that usually concludes the list
of posts and honorary titles.

Of all of these, *pontifex maximus* and *pater patriae* were titles the emperor usually received upon accession and then held for life. The consulship and *tribunicia potestas*, on the other hand, were yearly renewable titles. While no emperor was consul each year, they did hold tribunician power annually, making this particular title the most convenient for dating inscriptions. The other titles can help us date particular inscriptions as well, since the years in which emperors acted as consuls are well documented in literary sources, as are the specific years in which an honorary title was awarded. For example, an inscription of Trajan only mentioning **GERM DAC** must have been put up between AD 102 and 114, as after that date his victory over the Parthians, and thus his title of **PARTH**, would have been included.

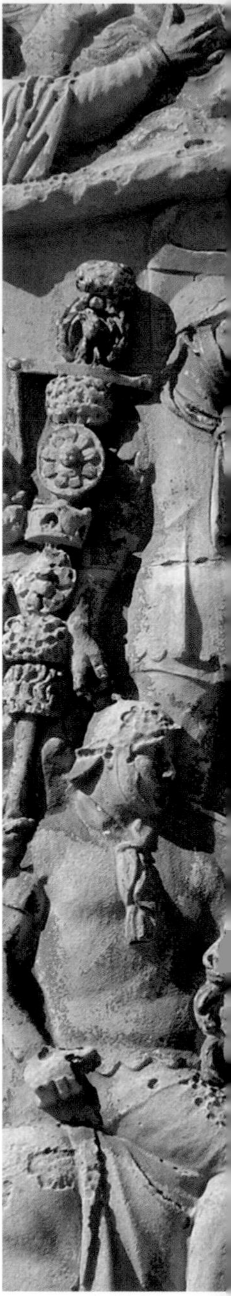

Fig. 12 Detail from Trajan's Column, a monument to commemorate Trajan's victories over the Dacians. The two Dacian Wars are depicted in comic-book style around the column.

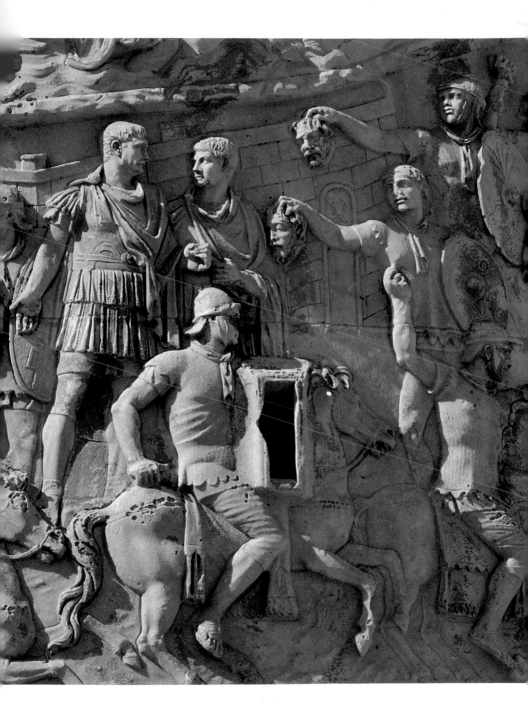

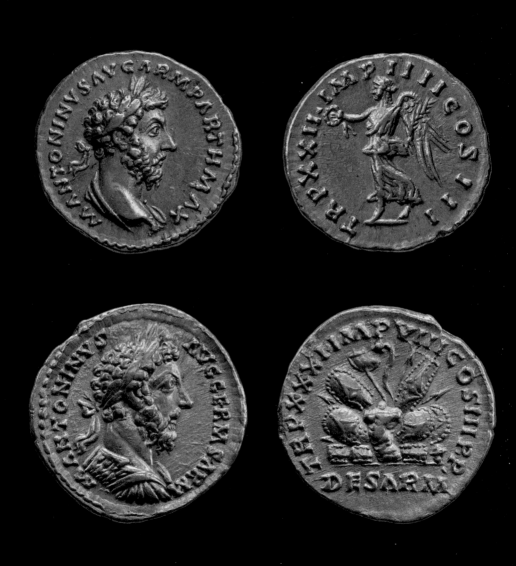

10

These gold coins of Marcus Aurelius (r. AD 161–80) show all the different titles he held at the time of minting, and can thus be very closely dated. The first one, showing the laureate head of the emperor, reads:
M ANTONINVS AVG ARM PARTH MAX (obverse) and
TR P XXII IMP IIII COS III (reverse).

The first line refers to the emperor as *Arm(eniacus)*, a title he was awarded in AD 164 after victory over the Armenians, and *Parth(icus) Max(imus)*, awarded in AD 166 after victory over the Parthians. On the reverse a representation of Victory emphasizes those military feats. We also learn that he held tribunician power for the 22nd time, was acclaimed imperator three times, and that he was consul for the third time. This dates the coin to AD 167–8. It is strange that *pater patriae* was not included, a title awarded to him in AD 166 – possibly this had something to do with space issues.

Upon the death of his co-emperor Lucius Verus in AD 169, Marcus dropped some of the titles that they had both held. However, in AD 172 he received the title *Germanicus*, following a victory in Germania, and in AD 175 the title *Sarmaticus*, after a victory over the Sarmatians, a people from north of the Black Sea. Thus the second coin reads:
M ANTONINVS AVG GERM SARM (obverse) and
TR P XXXI IMP VIII COS III P P (reverse).

It depicts Sarmatian armour as booty, including cuirass, shields, helmets and spears. Also featured are a *draco*, a dragon standard carried into battle by Dacian and Sarmatian soldiers, and the legend **DE SARM**(*atia*), meaning '(Victory) over Sarmatia'. Now in the 31st year of tribunician power, as well as imperator for the eighth time, consul for the third and *pater patriae*, this coin can be dated to AD 176–7.

The same titles and their abbreviations we see on this coin can be found on inscriptions on stone.

11

IMP · CAESAR · [[---------------
---------]] S · PONTIF · MAXIMVS · TRIB
POTEST · COS · XV · CENSOR · PERPETVS · P · P
PONTEM · A SOLO · FECIT
[[------------------]]
Q · LICINIO · ANCOTIO · PROCVLO · PRAEF · CAST
L · ANTISTIO · ASIATICO · PRAEF · BEREN ·
CVRA · C · IVLI · MAGNI · 7 · LEG · III CYR

Imp(erator) Caesar [[Domitianus Aug(ustus)]] / [[Germanicu]]s pontif(ex)
maximus trib(uniciae) / potest(atis) co(n)s(ul) XV censor perpetu<u>s p(ater)
p(atriae) / pontem a solo fecit
[[----------------]]
Q(uinto) Licinio Ancotio Proculo Praef(ecto) cast(rorum) / L(ucio) Antistio
Asiatico Praef(ecto) Beren(ices) / cura C(aii) Iuli Magni (centurionis) leg(ionis)
III Cyr(enae)

The emperor Caesar [erased: Domitianus Augustus Germanicus], chief priest,
holding tribunician power, consul for the 15th time, censor for life and pater
patriae, *built this bridge (*pontem*) from the foundations (*a solo*).*
[erased: M. Mettius Rufus, being Prefect of Egypt,]
Quintus Licinius Ancotius Proculus being Prefect of the (military) camps and
Lucius Antistius Asiaticus being Prefect of (the port of) Berenice. The project was
overseen by Gaius Iulius Magnus, centurion in the 3rd Legion 'Cyrenaica'.

This inscription, which was found in Coptos, Egypt and was set up to
commemorate the building of a bridge by the Roman army, shows the
name and titles of the emperor Domitian. Since he is called *Germanicus*, the
inscription certainly dates to post-AD 83, when this title was awarded to him,
and because his 15th consulship is mentioned we can more securely date it
to AD 90/91. Domitian was the only emperor to take the censorate for life,
as it is labelled here.

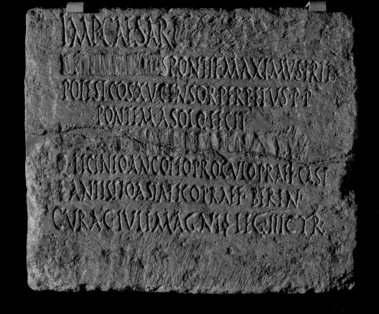

Immediately noticeable and of particular interest is the double erasure of names on this slab. Erasing names from inscriptions was part of the *damnatio memoriae*, the 'condemnation of the memory', a punishment that could be handed out by the emperor or Senate. The first erasure to have happened here was that of the name of the Prefect of Egypt, Marcus Mettius Rufus, by order of Domitian himself (we do not know why). Mettius Rufus, who was even mentioned by Suetonius (Suet. *Dom.* 4), was prefect, **PRAEF**(*ectus*), there between AD 89 and mid-AD 91, which means his name must have been erased very shortly after the stone was set up. Ironically Domitian suffered the *damnatio memoriae* himself after his murder (in all, over 30 emperors would suffer this fate), so his name was erased as well, in or shortly after AD 96. Despite this, the monumental inscription remained standing by the bridge it commemorated.

See inscription 14 for the 7-shaped symbol that represents the word 'centurion'.

To rule an empire, the emperor of course relied on a multitude of different magistrates and officials, both in Rome and abroad. A political career in Rome was profoundly formalized. A defined path of both military and political offices, all of which had to be held in a particular order and were subject to a minimum age, led towards the holder becoming consul, the highest possible magistrate. This career path was called the *cursus honorum*, literally the 'course of offices'. These were, in chronological order: military tribune, **TRIB**(*unus*) **MIL**(*itum*); quaestor, **QVAEST**(*or*) or just **Q**; aedile, **AED**(*ilis*) or **AEDIL**; praetor, **PRAET**(*or*) and finally consul, **COS**, at the minimum age of forty-two. After completing either the praetorship or the consulship one could become governor of one of the provinces, **LEG**(*atus*) **PRO PR**(*aetore*); and after the consulship specifically, one could become a censor (see above).

Completion of the entire *cursus* was a point of pride, especially if completed 'in time'; in reality, however, careers could take many different paths while aspiring for the consulship. Some inscriptions show a perfect run of the *cursus honorum*, but sometimes by the time a magistrate died he had held so many more and different posts, more prestigious and important than the earlier ones, that the latter were omitted.

Fig. 13 The Via Sacra, Ephesus, Turkey, along which the tomb of Marcus Helvius Geminus was located (see inscription 12, p. 62).

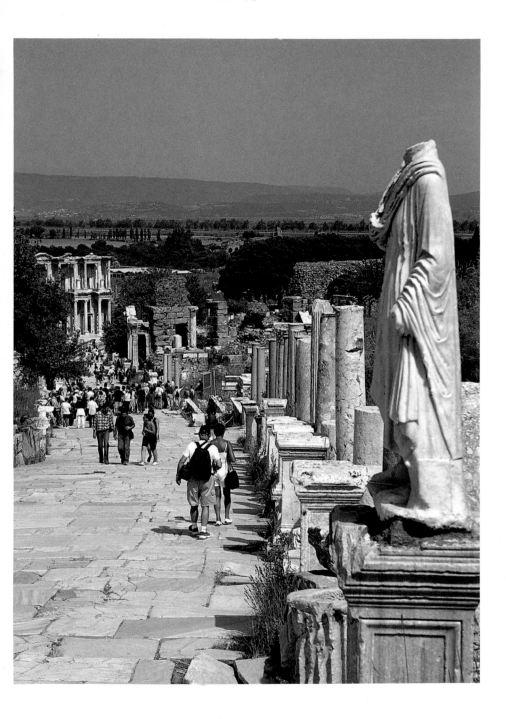

M · HELVIO · L · F · FAL
GEMINO · II VIR · A · A · A
F · F · SALIO · PALATINO · TRIB
MILIT · LEG · XVI · GERMANIAE
Q · CAESARIS · PRAET · LEG · MACED
PRO · PR · LEGA · SIA · ET · PRO · PRAET
ADLECTO · INTER · PATRICIOS · A
DIVO · CLAVDIO

12

M · HELVIO · L · F · FAL
GEMINO · III · VIR · A · A · A ·
F · F · SALIO · PALATINO · TRIB
MILIT · LEG · XVI · GERMANIAE
Q · CAESARIS · PRAET · LEG · MACED
PRO · PR · LEG · ASIAE · PRO · PRAET
AD · LECTO · INTER · PATRICIOS · A
DIVO   CLAVDIO

M(arco) Helvio L(ucii) f(ilio) Fal(erna) / Gemino ((trium))vir(o) a(ere) a(rgento) a(uro) / f(lando) f(eriundo) salio Palatino trib(uno) / milit(um) leg(ionis) XVI Germaniae / q(uaestori) Caesaris praet(ori) leg(ato) Maced(oniae) / pro pr(aetore) leg(ato) Asiae pro praet(ore) ad lecto inter patricios a / divo Claudio

(Dedicated) to Marcus Helvius Geminus, son of Lucius, of the Falerna voting tribe, moneyer, Salian priest of the Palatine priesthood of Mars, military tribune of the 16th Legion 'Germania', personal quaestor to the emperor, praetor, governor of the province of Macedonia, governor of the province of Asia, elevated to the class of patricians by the deified Claudius.

This inscription was set up on the outside of a monumental tomb on the Via Sacra at Ephesus, the main processional route of the city, where it was thus seen by thousands of people each year. The career of Marcus Helvius Geminus is an almost perfect *cursus honorum*. Starting out with minor positions as moneyer (lit.: **IIIVIR A A A F F**, 'one of three men for striking and casting bronze, silver and gold coins') and priest in one of the prestigious priesthoods in Rome (*salius Palatinus*), he became military tribune, quaestor and then praetor, although apparently not aedile. He also does not appear to have made it to consul, however, but was twice governor of a province.

These were prestigious posts, yet Geminus chose not to record them as the final, and thus most prominent, position in the inscription. Instead he emphasized the deified emperor Claudius, as his elevation among the patrician class, the Roman aristocracy, by Claudius, an event that we know happened in AD 48, was the start of Geminus's career. Using this date as the earliest possible starting point of his career, Geminus's quaestorship and governorships must have happened under Nero. He died in the province of Asia during his last governorship, and was thus buried in a very prominent place in Ephesus, then capital of that province.

A potential confusion might arise between the three times that **LEG** appears in this inscription – first as abbreviation for *legio*, as in the previous inscription, and then twice as abbreviation for *legatus*. In cases such as these it is always necessary to look at what follows. Legions nearly always have the abbreviation LEG preceding the specific number and name of the legion. Examples are **LEG VI VICTRIX**, the Sixth Legion 'Victorious', which was stationed in York during the second century AD and helped build Hadrian's Wall, or the **LEG I GERMANICA**, the first Legion 'Germanica', which had distinguished itself in the province of Germania under Augustus. Throughout Roman history dozens of different legions came into existence (a full list would be too long to produce here); several of them shared the same numeral, but none the same name. Similarly **LEG** for *legatus* will always need further specification, as in this instance: *legatus pro praetore* for specific provinces.

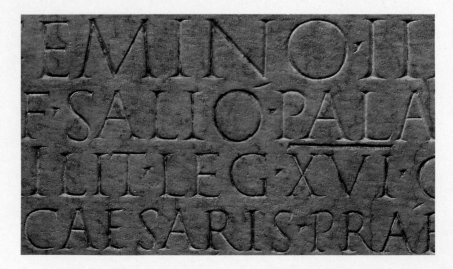

The legwork in ruling an empire was not, of course, done by politicians, but by the vast army that the emperor and the Senate could rely upon. It was made up of thousands of soldiers, both Roman and foreign. The abbreviations **MIL** and **MILIT** can stand for both *miles*, 'soldier', and *militare*, 'serve in the army'. The context usually makes clear which one is being used, as in the next inscription, but even if it does not, their differences are not likely to cause much confusion. Roman citizenship brought a whole range of benefits with it, and for many foreigners in the early Empire, serving in the army was the main, or only, possible way of being granted that citizenship after twenty-five years of service. We thus find a wide array of different nationalities in the inscriptions of the soldiers of the fleet and infantry, almost always starting with **NAT**(*ione*). These identities were expressed in several ways, including provinces, cities and tribes, such as *Delmata*, from the province Dalmatia; *Bessus*, from the Thracian tribe of the Bessi; *Afer*, from the province Africa Proconsularis; *Arabo*, meaning Arabic-speaking; *Graecus*, Greek (though the province was called Achaea); *Alex* or *Alexandri*, from the city of Alexandria; *Sinop*, meaning from the city of Sinope in modern-day Turkey, and more.

Only through the funerary inscriptions of ordinary soldiers do we get detailed information about their careers, as their years of service and their rising in the ranks were obvious points of pride. A dozen or so surviving plaques from a single *columbarium* at Misenum, a town near Naples where the imperial naval fleet (*classis*) was stationed, inform us about the age and specific tasks of those they commemorate, and even which ships they served on. Most of the plaques carry the inscription **CL · PR · MIS(EN)**, for *classis praetoria misenensis*, 'the praetorian fleet at Misenum'. The other part of the imperial fleet was kept at Ravenna (hence the modern name of the famous church of Sant'Apollinare in *Classe*), and was abbreviated to **CL · PR · RAVENN.**

13

D · M ·
C · IVLIO ARISTONI MILITI
CL · PR · MISEN · LIB · NEREIDE
AEGYPTIO · MILIT · ANN · XIIII
VIXIT · ANN · XXXV · C · ARRVN
TIVS · VALENS · OPTIO · EX EADEM
HERES · B · M ·

D(is) M(anibus) / C(aio) Iulio Aristoni militi / (ex) cl(asse) pr(aetoria)
Misen(ensi) lib(urna) Nereide / Aegyptio milit(avit) ann(is) XIIII / vixit ann(is)
XXXV C(aius) Arrun/tius Valens optio ex eadem / heres b(ene) m(erenti) (fecit)

To the Spirits of the Dead. To Gaius Iulius Ariston, soldier on the liburna **Nereis**
*of the praetorian fleet at Misenum, of Egyptian origin. He was a soldier for 14
years and lived for 35. Gaius Arruntius Valens, optio in the same section and his
heir, (made this) to him, well-deserving.*

This epitaph was made by Gaius Arruntius Valens. He was *optio* (second-in-command) of the same military section (*ex eadem*) as the person he made it for,
Gaius Iulius Ariston, whose name (on the second line) and dedication (*bene
merenti*, on the last line) are in the dative, as it was dedicated to him. Valens was
also Ariston's heir (*heres*). Ariston himself was a low-ranking, ordinary soldier
(*miles*, dative: *militi*) of the small galley *Nereis* (*liburna Nereide*) in the praetorian
fleet at Misenum (*ex classe praetoria Misenensi*). He was Egyptian by birth
(*Aegyptio*) and served as a soldier (*militavit*) for 14 years; he lived for 35 years.

The inscription offers a glimpse into the private, daily life of soldiers in the
Roman army. We can deduce that a certain bond existed, not just between
soldiers of the same rank but also extending to commanders, who took care
of their subordinates. In this case Ariston even makes his superior his heir,
perhaps indicating that he was not in touch with his parents (or they were
dead) and he had never married – in theory soldiers were not allowed to
marry while serving, but in practice the rules were often much more relaxed.

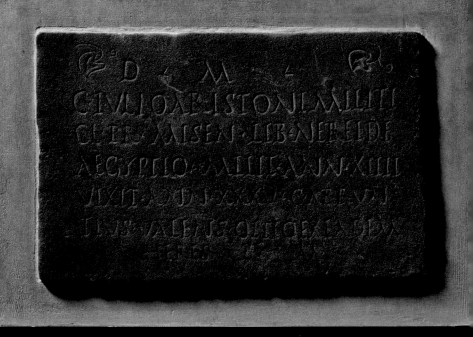

We also learn of individual names of vessels within the fleet. In this case the *liburna* was aptly named *Nereis*, Latin for Nereid, a sea nymph in Greek and Roman mythology. The other inscriptions from Misenum teach us the names of other vessels, always charged with significance: *Spes* ('Hope'), *Victoria* ('Victory'), *Pinnata* ('Winged'), as well as other mythological creatures, such as Triton and Oceanus, or any of the sea gods, as inscription 14 makes clear.

14

D · M ·
M · NAEVIO · PROCVLO
OPT · CONV · IIII · VENER
MIL · ANN · III · QVI · VIX · AN
XXI · M · II · D · XV · PARENTES
FILIO · DVLCISSIMO

D(is) M(anibus) / M(arco) Naevio Proculo / opt(ioni) conv(alescentium)
((quadriere)) Vener(e) / mil(itavit) ann(is) III qui vix(it) an(nis) / XXI m(ensibus)
II d(iebus) XV parentes / filio dulcissimo

To the Spirits of the Dead. To Marcus Naevius Proculus, who was in charge
*(*optio, *as above) of the recovering soldiers on the quadrireme Venus (*IIII, *which*
stands for Latin quadrieris, *ablative in –e;* Venere, *ablative of Venus), who*
soldiered for 3 years and who lived for 21 years, 2 months and 15 days. His
parents (set up this epitaph) to the sweetest of sons (dative filio dulcissimo*).*

The *optio convalescentium* ran the sick room for recovering soldiers. Military
funerary inscriptions inform us of many more different categories and
functions of both higher and lower ranking soldiers, about whom the literary
sources often remain silent: **VET***(eranus)* for a retired soldier; a **7**-like symbol
for either a *centurion* or a century (as seen in inscription 11, p. 58); **SIGNIF***(er)*
for standard-bearer (see inscription 15, p. 70); **ARM** or **ARMOR** for *armorum*
custos, armourer, or keeper of the weapons; **ADIVTOR TR** for *adiutor*
trierarchus, attendant to the trierarch, the captain of the trireme; **GYB(ER)** or
GVB(ER) for *gubernator*, helmsman; and even **NAVF** for *nauphilax*, luggage
guard.

Venus can be considered quite a prestigious name for a vessel, one that
hopefully was to bring good luck: after all, Venus herself had been born from
the sea. At first sight the use of **IIII** as quadrireme, just as **III** was used for
trireme (*trieris*) can be difficult to distinguish from the use of a numeral as a
time scale (such as age at death), or from anything else using numerals.

D · M ·
M·NAEVIO·PROCVLO
OPT·CONV·IIII·VENER
MIL·ANN·III·QVI·VIXAN
XXI·M·II·D·XV·PARENTES
FILIO·DVLCISSIMO
PRESENTED BY THO. HOLLIS. 1757.

However, if used as time, it will always be preceded by an abbreviation for 'years' (see p. 36). Similarly, when confronted with the titles and military functions preceding **LIB** in the previous inscription, one understands that it can hardly be an abbreviation for *libertus*. Inscriptions such as these which mention vessel names of the fleet are very typical yet very rare, so there is usually little scope for confusion.

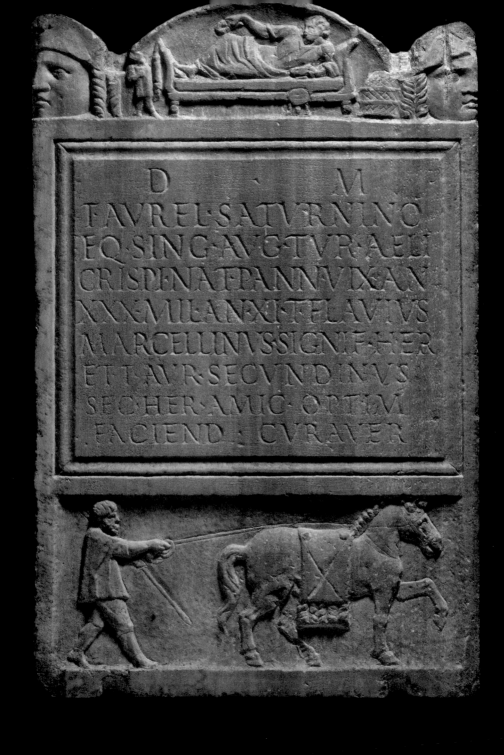

D · M

T·AVREL·SATVRNINO
EQ·SING·AVG·TVR·AELI
CRISPINATPANNVIXAN
XXX·MILANXITFLAVIVS
MARCELLINVSSIGNIFHER
ETTAVRSECVNDINVS
SECHERAMICOPTIM
FACIEND·CVRAVER

15

**D · M
T · AVREL · SATVRNINO
EQ · SING · AVG · TVR · AELI
CRISPI · NAT · PANN · VIX · AN
XXX · MIL · AN · XI · T · FLAVIVS
MARCELLINVS · SIGNIF · HER
ET · T · AVR · SECVNDINVS
SEC · HER · AMIC · OPTIM
FACIEND · CVRAVER**

D(is) M(anibus) / T(ito) Aurel(io) Saturnino / eq(uiti) sing(ulari) Aug(usti) tur(mae) Aeli / Crispi nat(ione) Pann(oniae) vix(it) an(nis) / XXX mil(itavit) an(nis) XI T(itus) Flavius / Marcellinus signif(er) her(es) / et T(itus) Aur(elius) Secundinus / sec(undus) her(es) amic(o) optim(o) / faciend(um) curaver(unt)

*To the Spirits of the Dead. To Titus Aurelius Saturninus, personal cavalryman of the emperor (*eques singularis Augusti*) in the squadron (*turma*) of Aelius Crispus and a native of the province of Pannonia. He lived for 30 years and was in the army for 11. Titus Flavius Marcellinus, standard-bearer and heir, and Titus Aurelius Secundinus, second heir (*secundus heres*), made sure that this (epitaph) was made (*faciendum curaverunt*) to their best friend (*amico optimo, in dative*).*

The *equites singulares* (plural of *eques singularis*) were cavalry bodyguards of high magistrates in the provinces, while the *equites singulares Augusti* (**EQ SING AVG**) were the cavalry branch of the Praetorian Guard, the personal bodyguards of the emperor. In AD 100 the Praetorian Guard numbered about 700, becoming closer to 2,000 around AD 200. Romans themselves were never great horse riders and therefore the cavalry, and specifically the *equites singulares,* were often recruited from among conquered foreigners, especially those from Germania, Dacia or, like Saturninus, from Pannonia (a province north-east of Italy).

The names of the three cavalrymen look problematic at first sight. Normally non-Roman soldiers would receive Roman citizenship only after 25 years of military service, but, as citizenship was obligatory for the Praetorians, the *equites singulares Augusti* received it upon recruitment. Naming conventions followed the normal standards, which means that they received the *praenomen* and *nomen* of the ruling emperors. Marcellinus seemingly received his citizenship under the Flavian emperor Titus (r. AD 79–81), yet Saturninus and Secondinus acquired theirs only under Antoninus Pius (born as Titus Aurelius; r. AD 138–61), which would put Marcellinus – rather implausibly – in active service for at least 58 years. A more feasible explanation is that Marcellinus had been freed by someone who had himself or herself received citizenship under a Flavian emperor, and thus probably entered the *equites singulares* as a citizen already.

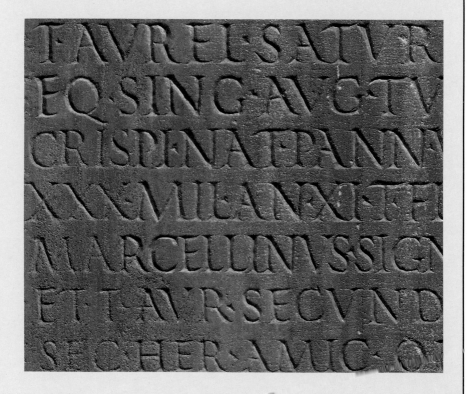

Wherever the army went, decent roads were necessary for swift movement and action, and soldiers would often be used, not always willingly, to build this extensive network. Milestones would be set up at regular intervals, and since roads were public works they would carry the reigning emperor's name and titles. This practice served not just to date and record the building of the road, but also to act as a propaganda device in the provinces – it is completely possible that, in the furthest corners of a vast empire, people were not always sure who the reigning emperor in faraway Rome might be.

Apart from those titles, the milestones record the distance one is removed from a certain place, inscribed as **A(B)**, 'from', plus the place name in the ablative case. The abbreviation **M P** was used for *milia passuum*, literally 1,000 paces, which equalled one mile. In Italy it was a given fact that any distance was recorded from Rome, so the city's name was omitted. In the provinces milestones usually stated the distance to the nearest large city or army camp. However, in line with the milestones' role in marketing the emperor's beneficence, the distance was subordinated to the titulature of the emperor, or other person responsible; on occasion we even find that distances and place names were not recorded. In a world where there were only a limited number of paved roads, however, it was probably considered more difficult to get lost, as long as one stayed on the road.

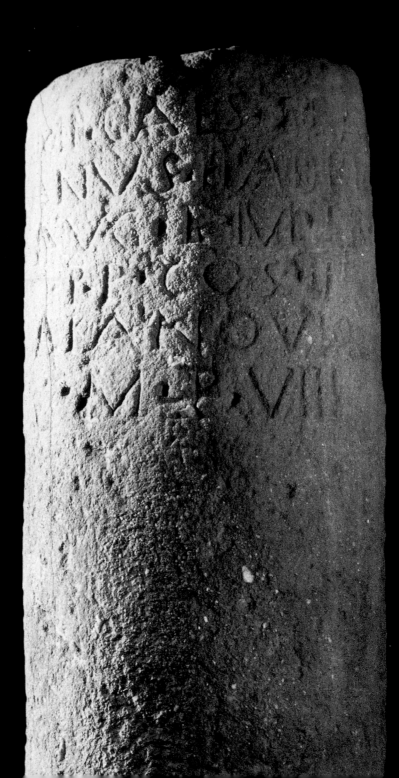

16

IMP · CAES · TRAI ANVS · HADRIANVS · AVG · P · M · TR · P · V · P · P · COS · III A · KANOVIO · M · P · VIII

Imp(erator) Caes(ar) Trai/anus Hadrianus / Aug(ustus) p(ontifex) m(aximus) tr(ibuniciae) p(otestatis) V / p(ater) p(atriae) co(n)s(ul) III / a Kanouio / m(ilia) p(assuum) VIII

The emperor Caesar Trajan Hadrian Augustus, chief priest, holding tribunician power for the fifth time, **pater patriae,** *consul for the third time. From Kanovium, 8 miles.*

This milestone was found in Wales at Llanfairfechan (Gwynedd) and is the earliest known milestone to survive from Roman Britain. It can be dated through Hadrian's fifth *tribunicia potestas* to between 10 December AD 120 and 9 December AD 121. The imperial titulature closely follows the conventions from Rome seen above, even when so far away as the outskirts of the province of Britannia.

It is one of five milestones discovered on the road between the military forts of Kanovium (Caerhun) and Segontium (Caernarfon, Gwynedd). Mention of an army camp on a milestone in this area is rare, indicating the importance Kanovium held at the time. Originally the lettering was painted red to stand out even more clearly and to be visible in bad weather, especially on a mountainous road such as this.

CHAPTER FIVE

Total Devotion

Sometimes inscriptions are accompanied by a figural relief that is never randomly chosen. Even the more generic ones, such as the Victories holding a funerary wreath on that of Lupercus (inscription 5, p. 30), were meaningful depictions within a funerary context, and occur over and over again. An extremely popular image was the representation of the deceased at a funerary banquet, as we find on Atimetus's funerary altar (inscription 4, p. 28). Other depictions made direct references to the deceased's life, most often representing a profession. On either side of Philomusus's grave relief (inscription 3, p. 26) is a *modius* (the left one inscribed with the word **MODI**), a measuring bucket for grain, indicating that Philomusus and his family were active in the grain trade. The bearded Saturninus, the cavalry bodyguard of the emperor, was depicted twice on his tombstone, once at a banquet and once while walking his horse (inscription 15, p. 70). Illustrations of many other professions can be found, including bakers, butchers, minters and civil servants and magistrates.

Fig. 14 Funerary relief
of a vegetable seller.
From Ostia, Italy,
c. 150–200.

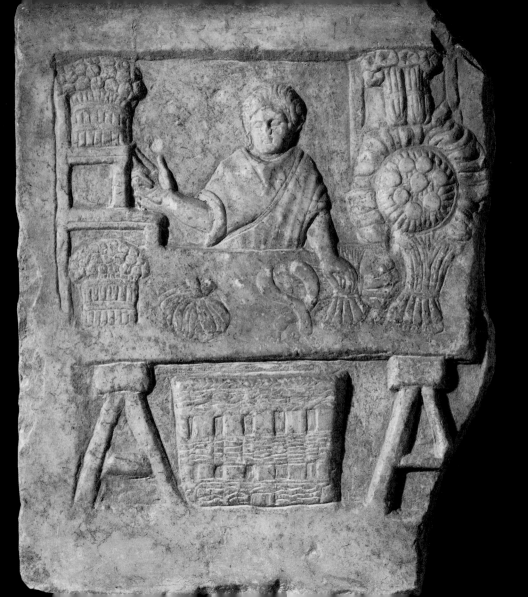

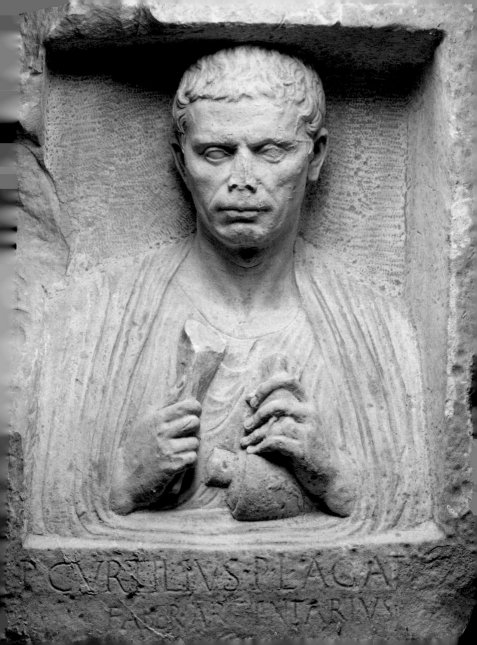

17

P · CVRTILIVS · P · L · AGAT
FABER · ARGENTARIVS

P(ublius) Curtilius P(ublii) l(ibertus) Agat(us) / faber argentarius

Publius Curtilius Agatus, freedman of Publius, silversmith

This freedman proudly showed himself on his tomb relief, not only sporting the typical Augustan hairstyle, wearing a toga (sign of his freed status) and an expensive looking ring but also holding the attributes of his trade that gave him his wealth and standing. With a mallet in his right hand and a chasing tool in his left, he is finishing the embossed decoration of a running satyr on a silver cup.

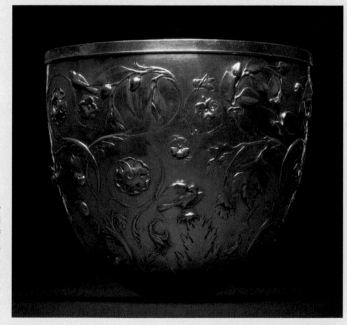

Fig. 15 A silver cup with embossed decoration of flowers, small birds and animals, which would have been made in the same way as shown on the relief opposite.

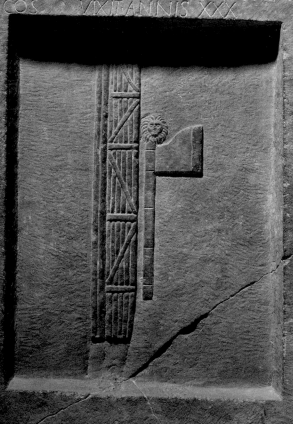

1283　D·PVBLICIVS
FRVCTVS·LICTOR·FONTEI·ACRIPPAE·PRO
COS.　VIXIT·ANNIS·XXX

18

**D · PVBLICIVS
FRVCTVS · LICTOR · FONTEI · AGRIPPAE · PRO
COS   VIXIT · ANNIS · XXX**

**D(ecimus) Publicius / Fructus lictor Fontei Agrippae pro/co(n)s(ulis)
vixit annis XXX**

*Decimus Publicius Fructus, lictor for the proconsul Fonteius Agrippa.
He lived for 30 years.*

The *fasces*, a bundle of wooden rods and an axe, are depicted on quite a few tombstones. They were carried by lictors such as Fructus, civil servants in charge of attending to and protecting most Roman magistrates, so basically the equivalent of a modern bodyguard.

Lictors were often freedmen. Their number depended on the rank of the magistrate: an aedile only had two, whereas a proconsul, as here, had 11. Consuls had 12, as originally did emperors, before Domitian increased their number to 24. A propraetor such as Helvius Geminus (inscription 12, p. 62) would have had five at his disposal.

Lictors had the power to punish and beat citizens with the *fasces* if they disturbed the magistrate or refused to get out of their way; they even had the power to execute. *Fasces* feature on tombstones of both lictors and of magistrates, sometimes in the same number as the lictors they were entitled to.

This tombstone was set up on the Magnesian Road, another of the processional roads of Ephesus (inscription 12, p. 62). Fonteius Agrippa became governor of the province of Asia in AD 69, the year in which Fructus must have served him and possibly died as well in active service. By AD 70 Agrippa had been transferred by the emperor Vespasian to the province of Moesia, where he was killed in battle shortly afterwards (as recounted in Tacitus, *Histories* 3.46 and Flavius Josephus, *Wars of the Jews* 7.4.3).

Votives and dedications to the gods

Dedications to the gods could happen for various reasons, either in order to ask for a favour, to repay a favour received or following a vision from a particular deity. Sometimes the sacrifices were recorded in inscriptions, and sometimes the inscriptions formed part of the object that was dedicated. Most of the time the name of the deity was all that was inscribed – in the dative case, as one was dedicating or giving to the god or goddess. However, other standardized expressions could expand upon the nature of the dedication. **D D** stood for *donum dedit*, 'gave as a gift', or *donum dedicavit*, 'dedicated this gift'. **V S** was short for *votum solvit*, 'fulfilled his/her vow', or *(ex) voto suscepto*, 'from the vow made'. Sometimes **V S L (L) M** was used, in which *libens (laetus) merito*, 'willingly, (gladly) and deservedly' was added to the former phrase. The longer expression was particularly prevalent in Roman Britain.

It should be noted that the actual favour for which a vow was made was seen as a private matter between god and supplicant, and therefore rarely mentioned. If the dedication was made following a divine vision, the words **EX VISU** or **EX VISO** were included, literally meaning 'because of/after a vision'. A specific type of supplication was for the wellbeing of other people, often, but not always, the emperor or members of the imperial family. Such prayers usually included the phrase **PRO SAL(VTE)**, 'for the wellbeing of'.

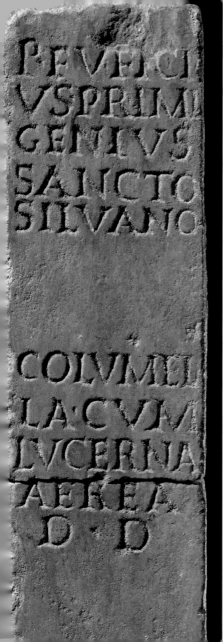

19

P · FVFICI
VS PRIMI
GENIVS
SANCTO
SILVANO

COLVMEL
LA · CVM
LVCERNA
AEREA
D · D

P(ublius) Fufici/us Primi/genius sancto Silvano / columel/la cum / lucerna / aerea / d(onum) d(edit)

Publius Fuficius Primigenius, to sacred Silvanus, this small column (columella) with a bronze lamp (lucerna aerea) he gave as a gift.

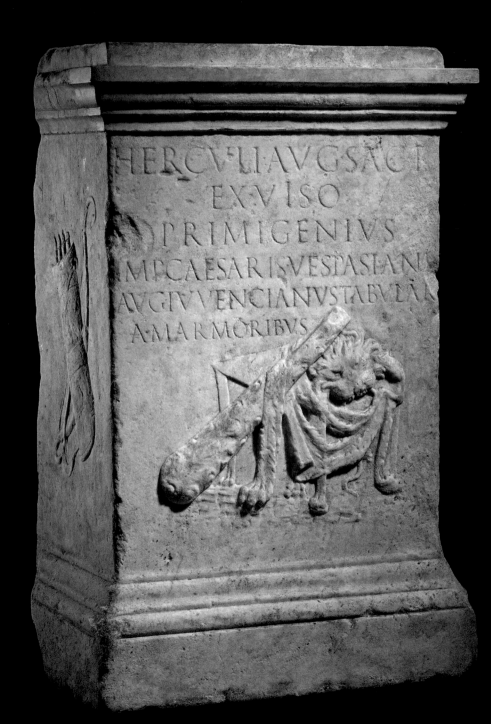

HERCVLIAVGSAC·
EX·VISO
PRIMIGENIVS
IMPCAESARISVESPASIANI
AVGIVVENCIANVSTABVLAR
A·MARMORIBVS

20

HERCVLI · AVG · SACR
EX · VISO
PRIMIGENIVS
IMP CAESARIS VESPASIANI
AVG · IVVENCIANVS TABVLAR
A · MARMORIBVS

Herculi Aug(usto) sacr(um) / ex viso / Primigenius / Imp(eratoris) Caesaris Vespasiani / Aug(usti) Iuvencianus tabular(ius) / a marmoribus

Sacred to Hercules, Protector of the Emperor, after a vision. Primigenius Iuvencianus, (slave or freedman) of the emperor Caesar Vespasian Augustus, book-keeper in the marble trade.

In both cases the inscription is recorded on the actual object that was dedicated to the god: a little stele and a large altar. Also in both cases, however, it was expected that frequent offerings would follow after the dedication. In the second inscription we learn who the dedicant was – Primigenius, a clerk in the marble trade of Rome. He was either a slave of the emperor (implied by the name of the emperor following in the genitive) or, more likely, one of his freedmen (he has at least two names and the means to dedicate an expensive altar).

The marble that Primigenius oversaw coming into Rome was probably destined for imperially funded projects. Given that he worked under Vespasian, Primigenius may have overseen the import of marble necessary for buildings such as the Colosseum. The relief on the altar shows a club and a lion skin, the attributes of Hercules, the god to whom the altar is dedicated.

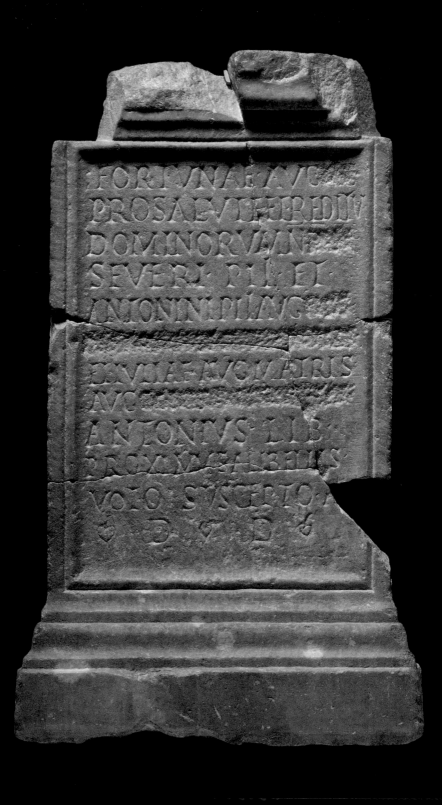

FORTVNAE AVG
PRO SALVTE ET REDITV
DOMINORVM N
SEVERI PII ET
ANTONINI PII AVG

......AE AVG MATRIS
AVG
ANTONIVS LIB
PROXIM... GABELLIS
VOTO SVSCEPTO
L M

21

FORTVNAE · AVG[[
PRO SALVTE · ET · REDITV
DOMINORVM · N[[
SEVERI · PII · ET ·
ANTONINI · PII · AVG[[
[[---]]
ET · IVLIAE · AVG · MATRIS
AVG [[---]]
ANTONIVS · LIB ·
PROXIMVS A LIBELLIS ·
VOTO · SVSCEPTO ·
D D

Fortunae Aug[[gg(ustorum)]] / pro salute et reditu / dominorum n[[nn(ostrorum)]] / Severi Pii et / Antonini Pii Aug[[g(ustorum) et]] / [[Getae Caesaris]] / et Iuliae Aug(ustae) matris / Aug[[gg(ustorum) et Plautillae Aug(ustae)]] / Antonius lib(ertus) / proximus a libellis / voto suscepto / d(onum) d(edit/edicavit)

To Fortuna, Protectress of the Emperors, for the wellbeing and (safe) return of our emperors Severus Pius [i.e. Septimius Severus] and Antoninus Pius [i.e. Caracalla] [erased: and prince Geta] and the empress Julia [i.e. Julia Domna], mother of the emperors (erased: and empress Plautilla). Antonius, freedman and imperial secretary for petitions, dedicated this gift, from a vow made.

As a *proximus a libellis*, the 'secretary for the petitions' to Septimius Severus, Antonius was a close assistant of the emperor, and it was expected of him to make vows and dedications of this type. The inscription on this votive stele indicates that he fulfilled the vow he made to Fortuna for the safe return of the imperial family.

Septimius Severus (r. AD 193–211) co-ruled with his son Caracalla between AD 198 and 211, and with his other son Geta between AD 209 and 211.

When Septimius died Caracalla ordered the assassination and *damnatio memoriae* of both his own wife Plautilla and his brother Geta, at which point their names were erased from this inscription.

In the case of two co-ruling emperors, the AVG in imperial titulature became **AVGG**, for the plural *Augusti*. Here, however, the AVGGG and NNN indicate three or more co-rulers, indicating that the empresses Julia Domna and Plautilla were included. This means that the inscription dates from the period between Caracalla's wedding to Plautilla in AD 202 and her early exile in AD 205. Strangely enough Julia Domna is named 'mother of the emperors', also followed by AVGGG, implying she was mother of three or more emperors. This must be a mistake from the part of whoever drew up the text, as many other inscriptions instead carry the correct title *'matris Aug(usti)'*, referring to her as mother of only Caracalla.

When the time came to erase the names from the inscription, the editor made the deliberate choice to erase all of the extra Gs and Ns, just leaving one for the sole ruler Caracalla. He should have left two, as one of them referred to the good Septimius Severus, who was not damned. It is likely that he simply did not want to take any risks under Caracalla.

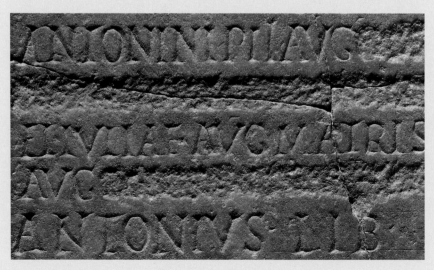

Affection

So far we have seen inscriptions that mainly use a fixed set
of phrases and abbreviations to convey a certain type of
information. Variation was possible, but almost exclusively
within a given framework. This was not a framework of
phrases imposed from above, but rather one that had
grown through the purpose of conveying as much
information as possible in as little space as necessary.
Standard ways of recording affection have appeared
throughout this book: *bene merenti*, 'well-deserving'; *amico
optimo*, 'to the dearest of friends'; *filio dulcissimo*, 'to the
sweetest of sons' and so on. Many were as applicable to
close family and friends as they were to beloved pets.

Exceptions were obviously possible, and we find that
these were mostly to emphasize affection as the dull flatness
of conventional phrases must have been all the more
painful to people in deep mourning. Sometimes, therefore,
heartfelt poems were inscribed, meant to be read by
passers-by to convey the deep loss that was felt by the death
of a loved one. For completeness and for their appeal these
inscriptions are given here, but in order to read them one
does need to understand a little more Latin.

D · M

DASVMIAE SOTERIDILI
BERTAE OPTIMAE ET CON
IVGI SANCTISSIMAE BENE
MER · FEC · L · DASVMIVS CAL
LISTVS CVM QVA VIX AN
XXXV SINE VLLA QVE
RELLA OPTANS VT IPSA
SIBI POTIVS SVPERSTES EV
ISSET QVAM SE SIBI SVPER
STITEM RELIQVISSET

22

D · M
DASVMIAE · SOTERIDI · LI
BERTAE · OPTIMAE · ET · CON
IVGI · SANCTISSIMAE · BENE
MER · FEC · L · DASVMIVS · CAL
LISTVS · CVM · QVA · VIX · AN
XXXV · SINE · VLLA · QVE
RELLA · OPTANS · VT · IPSA
SIBI · POTIVS · SVPERSTES · FV
ISSET · QVAM · SE · SIBI · SVPER
STITEM · RELIQVISSET

D(is) M(anibus) / Dasumiae Soteridi li/bertae optimae et Con/iugi sanctissimae bene / mer(enti) fec(it) L(ucius) Dasumius Cal/listus cum qua vix(it) an(nis) / XXXV sine ulla que/rella optans ut ipsa / sibi potius superstes fu/isset quam se sibi super/stitem reliquisset

Lucius Dasumius Callistus (dedicated this) to Dasumia Soteris, an excellent freedwoman and most virtuous, well-deserving wife, with whom he lived for 35 years with no cause for complaint, hoping that she would have outlived him, rather than that he, forsaken by her, would survive her.

The inscription is a mixture of two traditions. It starts by following the standardized rules for commemorating a deceased person, with names and status, through which we learn Dasumia was Dasumius's former slave, whom he freed and then married. The text then turns into a powerful eulogy and lamentation by Dasumius for his wife. No expense was spared as the text used no abbreviations, apart from *bene merenti*, *fecit* and *vixit*. We can still see a pair of feet which were part of the image of Dasumia, though the rest of the figure is missing. The large unworked area underneath the inscription, on the other hand, implies that Dasumius himself had left that space for his own funerary text. Why it was never recorded remains unknown.

23

Gallia me genuit nomen mihi divitis undae
concha dedit formae nominis aptus honos
docta per incertas audax discurrere silvas
collibus hirsutas atque agitare feras
non gravibus vinc(u)lis unquam consueta teneri
verbera nec niveo corpore saeva pati
molli namque sinu domini dominaeque iacebam
et noram in strato lassa cubare toro
et plus quam licuit muto canis ore loquebar
nulli latratus pertimuere meos
sed iam fata subii partu iactata sinistro
quam nunc sub parvo marmore terra tegit
Margarita

*Gaul gave me my birth and the pearl-oyster from the seas full of treasure my
name, an honour fitting to my beauty.
I was trained to run boldly through strange forests
and to hunt out furry wild beasts in the hills,
never accustomed to be held by heavy chains,
nor endure cruel beatings on my snow-white body.
I used to lie on the soft lap of my master and mistress
and when tired, knew to go to bed on my spread mattress
and I did not speak more than allowed as a dog, given a silent mouth.
No-one was scared by my barking,
but now I have been overcome by death from an ill-fated birth
and earth has covered me beneath this small piece of marble.
Margarita ('Pearl')*

A few tombstones for pet dogs survive from Roman times, but none as elaborate
and detailed as this one. The poem is written in verse and as if spoken by
Margarita, 'Pearl', herself. Dogs from Gaul were especially prized in antiquity
as hunting dogs as well as pets – both aspects that are covered in the verse.

GALLIA ME GENVIT NOMEN MIHI DIVITIS VNDAE
CONCHA DEDIT FORMAE NOMINIS APTVS HONOS
DOCTA PER INCERTAS AVDAX DISCVRRERE SILVAS
COLLIBVS HIRSVTAS ATQVE AGITARE FERAS
NON GRAVIBVS VINCLIS VNQVAM CONSVETA TENERI
VERBERA NEC NIVEO CORPORE SAEVA PATI
MOLLI NAMQVE SINV DOMINI DOMINAEQVE IACEBAM
ET NORAM IN STRATO LASSA CVBARE TORO
ET PLVS QVAM LICVIT MVTO CANIS ORE LOQVEBAR
NVLLI LATRATVS PERTIMVERE MEOS
SED IAM FATA SVBII PARTV IACTATA SINISTRO
QVAM NVNC SVB PARVO MARMORE TERRA TEGIT

MARGARITA

The poem shows the important role Margarita played in her owner's life through its quality and intellectual content. Several lines are plays on phrases from the most famous and respected Roman authors: *Gallia me genuit* reminded readers of Virgil's funerary epitaph *Mantua me genuit*, while other lines evoke Ovid's *The Art of Love* (line 8 – Ovid, *Ars Amatoria* 2, 370) and *The Art of Beauty* (line 12 – Ovid, *Medic.* 8) – good sources of inspiration for describing Margarita's qualities and the loss that her owners felt at her death.

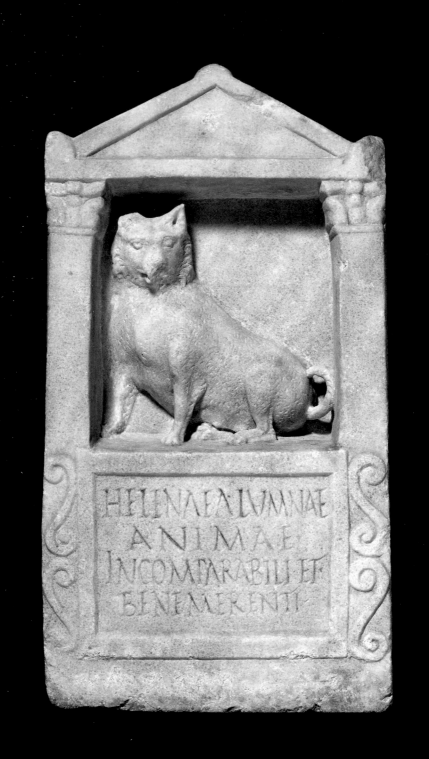

HELENAE ALVMNAE
ANIMAE
INCOMPARABILI ET
BENEMERENTI

24

HELENAE ALVMNAE
ANIMAE ·
INCOMPARABILI · ET ·
BENE · MERENTI ·

Helenae alumnae / animae / incomparabili et / bene merenti

To Helena, (our) nursling, an incomparable and well-deserving soul

From its depiction we know that Helena was an ancient miniature lapdog, a so-called Melitan, which featured often in Greek and Roman art. If the love that the family felt for Helena did not show enough through the small marble funerary shrine they set up for her, her name made it even clearer, for it recalls Helen of Troy, the most beautiful woman in the world. Here, however, the pet is shown in old age, tired, resting, and with a fat, weighing-down belly.

CHAPTER SIX

The Art of the Stonemason

So far we have discussed several different reasons for putting up inscriptions and analysed the individual texts. However, it is also worthwhile to consider the actual processes behind selecting, commissioning and buying an inscribed object. In a similar way to today, there were different suppliers involved. One workshop of stonemasons (*officina lapidaria*) would have been responsible for providing the actual object, e.g. an altar, while another might have provided the actual inscribing, performed by a *sculptor* or a *scriptor titulorum*; advertising signs of such workshops survive from different places in the Empire.

Choosing an inscription was always a negotiation between carver and client. Most stonemasons would display samples of their work, and even have pre-prepared slabs available, to which just a name could be added; they would also discuss the buyers' preferences to emphasize certain aspects in each inscription. We can imagine that some people chose to compose the inscriptions themselves, which certainly must have been the case for the more personal and poetic ones, such as those to Dasumia Soteris or to Margarita (inscriptions 22 and 23).

When looking at different inscriptions, we can see an enormous variety in quality between them. Some workshops were obviously more skilled than others, but also likely to have been more costly, so quality was closely linked to how much money one wanted or was able to spend. Equally the length of an inscription would depend upon the funds available, as stone was paid for by size and the stonemason paid for either by the letter or at an hourly rate. It is therefore not surprising to find such an advanced system of abbreviations in use throughout the Roman Empire. Not only does it signal the enormous bureaucracy that was inherent to the Romans, but it also just made economic sense.

Before a stonemason started to carve, it was necessary to lay out the text on the stone. Faint lines were carved at regular intervals to indicate the height of each row of letters, while the letters themselves were often painted or drafted with chalk or charcoal. Only then could the mason go to work. Many of these lines remain visible on the stones today, as they were not considered visible enough to disturb the reading. Even small plaques with only two lines of inscription could be created by laying out these lines, as one can see on the inscription by Sontius Philostorgus (fig. 7).

Another very good example is provided by the tombstone to Margarita (inscription 23, p. 92). Looking closely at the inscription, one can still make out these faintly carved horizontal lines. In addition we can also perceive vertical lines on the left hand side of the slab, up to about a third into it. While at first sight these could have been laid out to indicate the horizontal spacing of each individual letter, it is quite clear that none of the letters actually respect them. More probably the carver had started to lay out rows on a slab, then realized the slab was not wide enough to contain the lines of the poem in an orderly manner. He thus decided to turn the slab through 90 degrees, and had to lay out new lines accordingly.

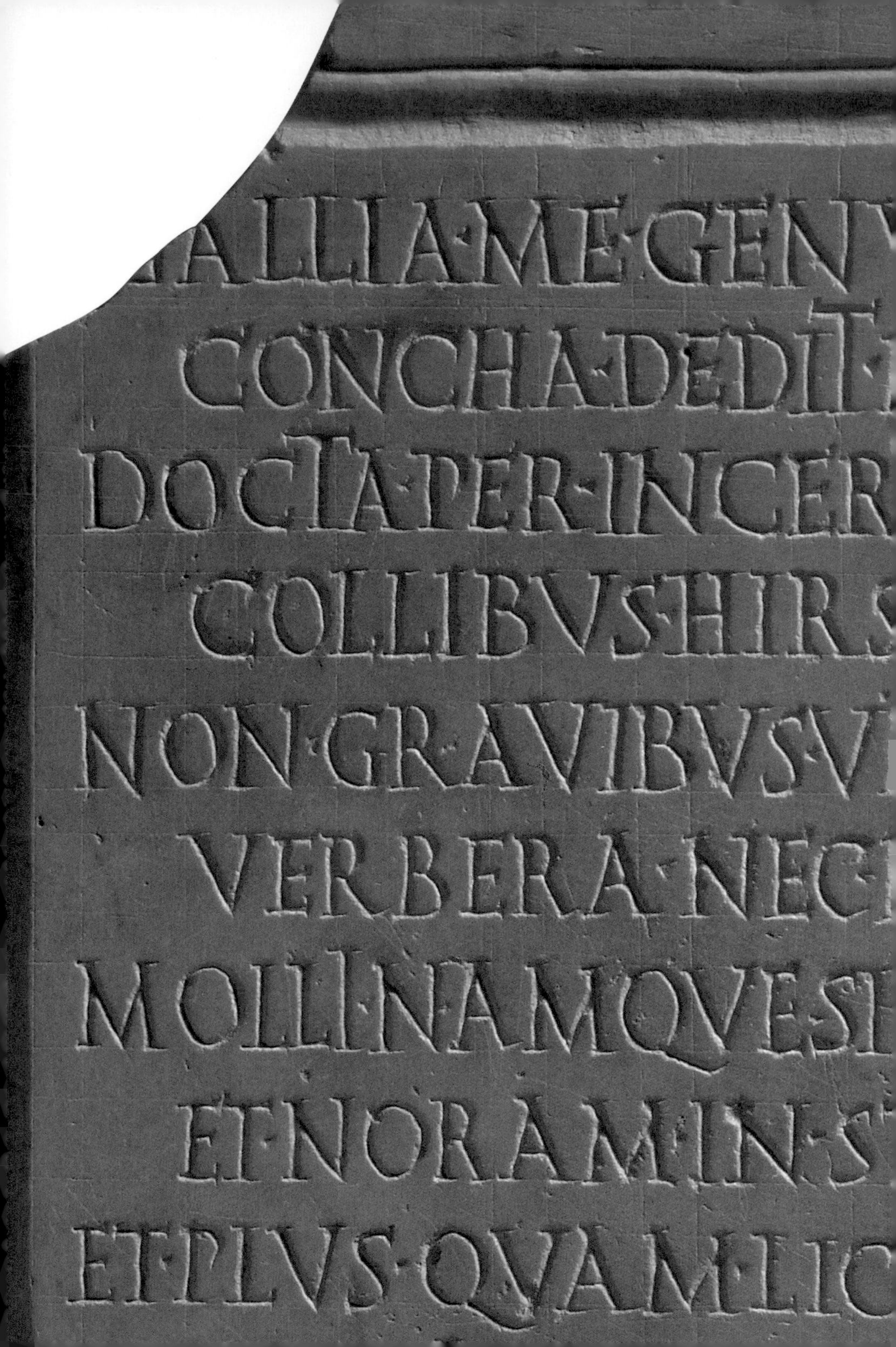

ALLIA ME GENV

CONCHA DEDIT

DOCTA PER INCER

COLLIBVS HIR S

NON GRAVIBVS V

VERBERA NEC

MOLLINAMQVE SI

ET NORAMIN S

ET PLVS QVAM LIC

There are obvious cases where this careful process was not applied and rows are not quite horizontal, as evident on the inscription of Decumius Vaarus (inscription 6, p. 32). This probably happened to inexperienced stonemasons, some of whom may have had no formal training, or indeed to the exact opposite: experienced carvers who no longer felt a need to bother with preparations. The latter must surely be the case for the otherwise beautifully carved inscription to Marcus Helvius Geminus at Ephesus (inscription 12, p. 62), which clearly shows the hand of a well-trained craftsman, with perfectly rounded capital lettering. Unfortunately three of the eight lines overrun the actual frame for the inscription, while the last two lines show a steady decline in quality. The overrunning is clearly due to the poor layout of the lettering before starting, though one wonders why the carver did not learn after the first line. However, it is harder to explain the difference in quality. Did whoever commissioned the stone change their mind about the order of titles? Or did another hand take over towards the end of the carving?

Strangely enough, mistakes in both spelling and grammar are extremely frequent in inscriptions, appearing in high-quality ones just as much as in those of lower standard. They are due to a variety of reasons. First and foremost is the fact that not every Roman was literate, and we should certainly not assume that every inscription carver could read and write himself. Stonemasons would work from a template and human error would sometimes slip in, either by whoever prepared the template or by the carver himself. This kind of simple error can be spotted in one of the *columbarium* epitaphs (fig. 9), where Flavia's name in dative is written as *Flaviai* instead of *Flaviae*. The use of –ai instead of the correct –ae is a very common error in inscriptions.

Even imperially commissioned inscriptions contain mistakes, however, such as *perpetus* for *perpetuus*, 'perpetual',

Fig. 16 Detail of the inscription for Margarita, showing two systems (one erroneously) of faint lines that were laid out before carving could start.

in the dedication of the bridge building in Egypt
(inscription 11, p. 58), and the intellectually more
challenging text for Margarita shows a grammatical
mistake at the very end, reading *teget* instead of *tegit* (see fig.
17, opposite). There are clear signs someone tried to correct
the mistake – perhaps the client spotted the mistake himself
when inspecting the finished product? A double mishap can
be spotted in the inscription to Fabius Superatus
(inscription 7, p. 38), where the word *vixit* shows both a later
correction, adding in a forgotten 'i', and an unconventional
spelling as *vixsit*. The latter is grammatically wrong, but it is
found in so many inscriptions that it is thought actually to
reflect the spoken Latin of the time and the region in which
this inscription was made, with an over-emphasized 's'
sound. Such phonetically written words occur all over the
empire throughout time, with the most common ones being
this very example of *vixsit* for *vixit* and a monophtong –e for
a diphthong –ae, e.g. *eterna* for *aeterna*, 'eternal', or an –i
instead of a –u, e.g. *monimentum* for *monumentum*.

Lastly mention should be made of ligatures. In order to
save space, as decoration, or perhaps as an intellectual
exercise, some inscriptions show long words contracted by
joining two or more letters together, or appearing as smaller
letters written within bigger ones. The meaning is often still
quite clear, as it is in the extreme example of inscription 25
(p. 102), on the tombstone of Marcus Cocceius Nonnius – a
young boy only six years old.

Fig. 17 Detail of the
inscription for
Margarita, showing the
corrected spelling
mistake in the last
word, turning *teget*
into *tegit*.

ATQVE IACEBAM

A RETORO

RELOQVEBAR

IEOS

TA SINISTRO

ORE TERRA FECIT

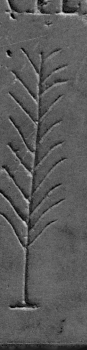

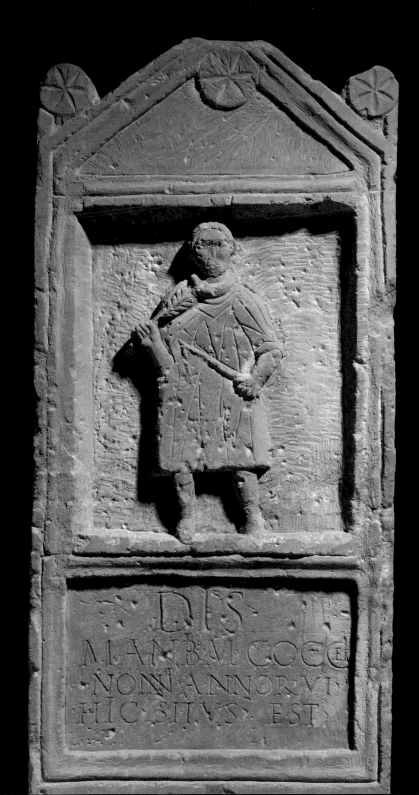

DIS
MANBAICOCCEI
NONNANNOR VI
HICSITVS EST

25

DIS
MANIB · M · COCCEI
NONNI · ANNOR · VI ·
HIC · SITVS · EST ·

Dis / Manib(us) M(arci) Coccei / Nonni annor(um) VI / hic situs est

To the spirits of the dead and of Marcus Cocceius Nonnus, 6 years (old).
He lies here.

The inscription shows two ligatures – the I and B in MANIB and the NNI of
NONNI – and one space-saving exercise, in which the E and I of COCCEI
are placed within the last C. Marcus is depicted himself in the relief, wearing
a tunic and holding a palm branch and whip. These attributes signify victory
in a chariot race, perhaps not necessarily implying that the little boy, who was
only six, had actually participated in any race, but just that he loved the sport.

Afterword

It is hoped that this brief overview has convinced the reader of the merit of studying Latin inscriptions. Rarely do remnants from the Roman world give us as much information about people's lives as these few words on stone. We hear the voices of slaves, women, children and emperors and can try to understand what was in their minds. What is immediately clear is that some of their lives and concerns seem very close to our own, while other aspects are difficult to imagine happening today. As a result of this deciphering, inscriptions can be both intriguing and fun. With this guide in hand any visit to a Roman museum, whether in Britain, Italy or elsewhere, will become a fascinating detective story.

Fig. 18 Detail of a watercolour by William Chambers, showing the sculpture collection of Charles Townley in the entrance hall of his house in Park Street, Westminster. A visitor is inspecting sculptures and inscriptions with the aid of Townley's handwritten guides.

Historical information, of course, increases our understanding of these snapshots from the past, so this book has tried to give as much of it as possible. Yet questions always linger. Why were two young boys with no apparent relationship buried together? Did one of them really live for exactly three years, three months and three days, or are we missing some mystical significance? Why was the title of Septimius Severus (inscription 21, p. 86) erased, if not by accident? Further study of inscriptions such as these continues to give us greater insight into the Roman world, and into the daily lives, emotions and feelings of the people who lived in it.

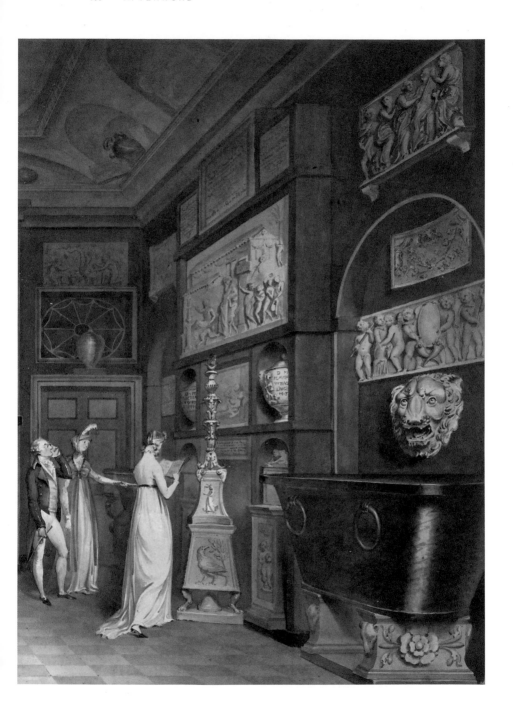

Roman emperors of the first two centuries AD

Augustus (born Octavius)	27 BC–AD 14
Tiberius	14–37
Caligula (Gaius)	37–41
Claudius	41–54
Nero	54–68
Year of the 4 emperors:	
Galba, Otho, Vitellius,	
Vespasian	68–69
Vespasian	69–79
Titus	79–81
Domitian	81–96
Nerva	96–98
Trajan	98–117
Hadrian	117–38
Antoninus Pius	138–61
Marcus Aurelius and **Lucius Verus**	161–69
Marcus Aurelius	161–80
– with **Commodus**	177–80
Commodus	177–92
Year of the 5 Emperors:	
Pertinax, Didius Julianus,	
Pescennius Niger, Clodius Albinus,	
Septimius Severus	193
Septimius Severus	193–211
– with **Caracalla**	198–211
– with **Caracalla** and **Geta**	209–11
Caracalla	198–217

List of Abbreviations

Note: Almost all abbreviations stay the same, whatever the case, number or person of the Latin word, e.g. ANN is used for *annum*, *annos*, *annis*, etc. or FEC for *fecit* and *fecerunt*.

7-like symbol, either a *centuria*, century (unit of 80/100 men in a legion) or a *centurion* (head of a *centuria*).

A(B), *a(b)*, from. If on a milestone often followed by a place name in the ablative case.

ABNEP(OS), *abnepos*, great-great-grandson.

ADIVTOR TR, *adiutor trierarchus*, attendant to the trierarch (the captain of a trireme).

AED, *aedilis*, aedile, a junior magistrate in charge of public works; sometimes with a further specification, such as

AED CVR, *aedilis curulis*, or **AED PLEB**, *aedilis plebis*.

AN or **ANN,** *annus*, year.

ARM or **ARMOR**, *armorum custos*, armourer/ keeper of the weapons.

AVG N, *Augustus noster*, our emperor.

AVG, Augustus or emperor.

AVGG, *Augusti*, used in times when more than one emperor ruled.

B M or **BENE MER(ENS)**, *bene merens*, well-deserving.

Ɔ, *Caia*, a woman.

CAES, *Caesar*.

CL PR MIS(EN), *classis praetoria Misenensis*, the praetorian fleet at Misenum.

CL PR RAVENN, *classis praetoria Ravennas*, the praetorian fleet at Ravenna.

COS, *consul*.

COS DESIG, *consul designatus*, someone appointed as consul, but not yet installed in post.

CVR, *curator*, in charge of public works; to be used with a specification, e.g. *curator aquarum*, in charge of Rome's aqueducts and water supply.

D D, *donum dedit*, gave as a gift, or *donum dedicavit*, dedicated this gift.

D M (S) or **DIS MANIBVS (SACRVM)**, *Dis Manibus (sacrum)*, (Sacred) To the Spirits of the Dead.

D S or **(DE) SVO** or **DE S P**, *de sua pecunia*, with his/her own money.

D(OM), *dominus*, master, used frequently for the emperors; also **D(OM) N**, *dominus noster*, our master.

D, *dies*, day.

DAC, *Dacicus*, honorific title after a victory over the Dacians.

DED, *dedicavit/dedicaverunt* (singular/plural), dedicated.

DIV, *divus*, deified/divine.

EQ SING AVG, *eques singularis Augusti*, the cavalry branch of the Praetorian Guard, the personal bodyguards of the emperor.

EX VISU or **EX VISO**, *ex visu/viso*, because of/ after a vision.

F C or **FAC CVR**, *faciendum curavit/curaverunt* (singular/ plural), made sure that (it) was made.

F or **FEC**, *fecit/fecerunt* (singular/plural), made this.

F or **FIL**, *filius/filia*, son/daughter.

GERM, *Germanicus*, honorific title after a victory over Germanic tribes.

GYB(ER) or **GVB(ER)**, *gubernator*, helmsman.

H M H N S, *hoc monumentum heredem non sequitur*, this tomb does not pass to my heir.

H S E S T T L, *hic situs/sita est, sit terra tibi levis*, he/ she lies here, may the earth rest lightly on you.

H S E, *hic situs/sita est*, he/she lies here (lit.: here is placed).

H, *hora*, hour.

II VIR, *duumvir*, member of any board of two magistrates performing a political function, often the two chief magistrates in a colony or municipality, similar to modern mayors. They shared authority, like the consuls in Rome. The abbreviation was sometimes followed with a further distinction, e.g. **II VIR I**(*ure*) **D**(*icundo*), for interpreting the law, a *duumvir* with judiciary authority.

III VIR, *triumvir*, member of any board of three magistrates performing a political function; often followed with a further distinction, such as **III VIR A A A F F**, *triumvir aere argento auro flando feriundo*, moneyer, lit. one of three men for striking and casting bronze, silver and gold coins.

III, *trieris*, trireme.

IIII VIR, *quattuorvir*, member of any board of four magistrates performing a political function; often followed with a further distinction.

IIII, *quadrieris*, quadrireme.

IMP, *imperator*, acclaimed by troops after a victory. During the Empire, it was exclusively used for the emperor.

IN F(R) P … IN A(GR) P …, *in fronte pedes …, in agro pedes …*, … feet wide, … feet deep.

L, *libertus/liberta* [m/f] freedman/woman.

LEG AVG PR PR, *legatus Augusti pro praetore*, governor of a province appointed by the emperor (lit. a former praetor whose office was extended to govern a province, specifically on behalf of the emperor).

LEG PR PR, *legatus pro praetore*, governor of a province (lit. a former praetor whose office was extended to governor of a province).

LEG, *legio*, legion.

LIB, *libertus/liberta* [m/f] freedman/woman.

LIB, *liburna*, a small galley.

LIBERTIS LIBERTABVSQVE, *libertis libertabusque*, to his/her freedmen and freedwomen.

LON P … LAT P …, *longum pedes … latum pedes, …* feet long, … feet wide.

M P, *milia passuum*, 1,000 paces, which equalled one mile.

M, *mensis*, month.

MIL or **MILIT**, *miles*, soldier, or *militavit/militaverunt* (singular/plural), served in the army.

NAT, *natione*, from the nation of.

NAVF, *nauphilax*, luggage guard.

NEP(OS), *nepos*, grandson; (sometimes for genitive and dative, **NEPTI(S)** is used instead of **NEPOTI(S)**); see also **PRONEP(OS)** and **ABNEP(OS)**, great-grandson and great-great-grandson.

P M / PONT MAX, *pontifex maximus*, the chief priest.

P P / PAT PAT, *pater patriae*, father of the fatherland.

PARTH, *Parthicus*, honorific title after a victory over the Parthians.

POS, *posuit/posuerunt* (singular/plural), placed.

POSTERISQVE EORVM, *posterique eorum*, to their descendants.

PR PR, *pro praetore*, with powers of a praetor.

PRAEF, *praefectus*, head of; to be used with a specification, e.g. *praefectus praetori*, originally the head of the Praetorian Guard, but eventually a more administrative function.

PRAET, praetor.

PRO, *provincia*, followed by the name of the province. If not it is probably part of the abbreviation for magisterial power, e.g. *pro praetore*, or *pro aedilitate*.

PRO SAL(VTE), *pro salute*, for the wellbeing of.

PROC, procurator, title for a wide variety of officials.

PROCOS, proconsul, governor of a province appointed by the Senate.

PRONEP(OS), *pronepos*, great-grandson.

Q / QVAEST, quaestor, a magistrate in the Roman system of government.

QVI VIX(IT), *qui vixit*, who lived.

S C or **(EX) S C**, *(ex) senatus consulto*, by decree of the Senate.

S E S L L P Q E, *sibi et suis libertis libertabusque posterisque eorum*, (made) for him/herself and his/her family and their descendants.

S S P E, *sibi et suis posterisque eorum*, (made) for him/herself and his/her family and to their descendants.

S T T L, *sit terra tibi levis*, may the earth rest lightly on you.

SAR, *Sarmaticus*, honorific title after a victory over the Sarmatians.

SER, *servus/serva* [m/f] slave.

SIBI ET SVIS LIBERTIS LIBERTABVSQVE POSTERISQVE EORVM, *sibi et suis libertis libertabusque posterisque eorum*, (made) for him/herself and his/her family and to his/her freedmen and freedwomen and their descendants.

SIGNIF, *signifer*, standard-bearer.

TR(IB) MIL, *tribunus militum*, military tribune.

TR(IB) PL, *tribunus plebis*, tribune of the people.

TRIB POT / TR P, *tribunicia potestas*, with powers of a tribune.

V S L (L) M, *votum solvit libens (laetus) merito*, fulfilled his/her vow, willingly, (gladly) and deservedly (a form particularly prevalent in Roman Britain).

V S, *votum solvit*, fulfilled his/her vow, or *(ex) voto suscepto*, from the vow made.

VERN(A) [m/f], *verna*, houseborn slave.

VET, *veteranus*, retired soldier.

VIX(IT), *vixit*, (he/she) lived.

Further Reading

Bruun, C. and Edmonson, J. 2015 *The Oxford Handbook of Roman Epigraphy*. New York

Cooley, A.E. 2012 *The Cambridge Manual of Latin Epigraphy*. Cambridge

Harvey, B.K. 2004 *Roman Lives: Ancient Roman Life as Illustrated by Latin Inscriptions*. Massachusetts

Keppie, L. 1991, 2001 *Understanding Roman Inscriptions*. Baltimore

LaFleur, R.A. 2010 *Scribblers, Sculptors, and Scribes: A Companion to Wheelock's Latin and Other Introductory Textbooks*. New York

Lansford, T. 2009 *The Latin Inscriptions of Rome: A Walking Guide*. Baltimore

Acknowledgements

During the last hundred years, several curators and scholars before me have attempted to properly catalogue the collection of Latin inscriptions on stone in the Department of Greece and Rome at the BM. This book is dedicated to all of those epigraphers that tried, even if it only shows a selection of a total of almost 450 inscriptions. They are interesting ones, but not the only interesting ones. All others are now consultable digitally on the Museum's Online Database.

Work on the catalogue, and thus indirectly on this book, was done tirelessly by several highly skilled volunteers: Dr Caroline Barron, Dr Alexandra Sofroniew, Dr Giulia Masci, and Dr Monica Pavese. However, James Wilson never allowed me to lose track of the fact that the majority of museum visitors are not academics. To him, I owe an accurate, yet still understandable translation of the Margarita inscription. Any errors in the final writing of the book of course remain my own.

Picture Credits

All images of British Museum objects are copyright the
Trustees of the British Museum and are courtesy of the
Photographic and Imaging Department.

Inscriptions

Dimensions are given in the order of height, width and depth.
All of the inscriptions with the depth given as 1 cm are set into
concrete blocks.

1: British Museum 1867,0508.67 (29 x 35 x 8.5 cm)

2: British Museum 1896,1024.1 (45.6 x 30.7 x 31.7 cm)

3: British Museum 1920,0220,1 (61.0 x 165.0 x 18.5 cm)

4: British Museum 1817,0208.2 (48 x 36 x 30cm)

5. British Museum 1817,0208.4 (32.0 x 42.0 x 34.5 cm)

6. British Museum 1973,0108,1 (42.5 x 71.5 x 4.1 cm)

7. British Museum 1905,1205.4 (28 x 21 x 2.5 cm)

8. British Museum 1896,1024.1 (45.6 x 30.7 x 31.7 cm)

9. British Museum 1756,0101.199 (34.5 x 59 x 1 cm)

10. British Museum 1856,1101.70 / THO,1815

11. British Museum 1894,1105.1 (58.5 x 67.5 x 14.5 cm)

12. British Museum 1867,1122.415 (57 x 95.5 x 12 cm)

13. British Museum 1973,0111.1 (21.5 x 33.5 x 1 cm)

14. British Museum 1757,0816.16 (23.6 x 33.0 x 3.0 cm)

15. British Museum 1896,0619.6 (96 x 60.5 x 5 cm)

16. British Museum 1883,0725.1 (170.0 x 44.0 x 47.0 cm)

17. Los Angeles, J. Paul Getty Museum, 96.AA.40 (79.9 x 58.5 x 31.7 cm)

18. British Museum, 1868,0620,55 (142 x 85 x 23 cm)

19. British Museum, 1986,0405.1 (26.5 x 7 x 7.5 cm)

20. British Museum, 1914,0627.1 (72 x 46 x 30 cm)

21. British Museum, 1805,0703.210 (81 x 47.5 x 8 cm)

22. British Museum, 1805,0703.202 (63.7 x 36.6 x 5.0 cm)

23. British Museum, 1756,0101.1126 (50 x 60.5 x 1 cm)

24. Los Angeles, J. Paul Getty Museum 71.AA.271 (61 x 31.5 cm)

25. British Museum, 1969,0701.4 (225.0 x 91.0 x 18.0 cm)

Figure Illustrations

Fig. 1 Superstock/ Universal Images Group

Fig. 2 © The Trustees of the British Museum

Fig. 3 © The Trustees of the British Museum, R.7949

Fig. 4 Giovanni Batista Piranesi, *Le Antichità Romane*, vol. 3, pl. LI.

Fig. 5 Araldo De Luca

Fig. 6 © The Trustees of the British Museum (drawing by Kate Morton)

Fig. 7 © The Trustees of the British Museum, 1900,0517.1

Fig. 8 © The Trustees of the British Museum, 1973,0108.87

Fig. 9 © The Trustees of the British Museum, 1973,0108.98

Fig. 10 © The Trustees of the British Museum, 1973,0108.2

Fig. 11 © The Trustees of the British Museum, 1973,0108.41

Fig. 12 Adam Eastland Rome/ Alamy Stock Photo

Fig. 13 Konrad Wothe/ Robert Harding

Fig. 14 Museo Ostiense © 2015. Photo Scala, Florence – courtesy of the Ministero Beni e Att. Culturali

Fig. 15 © The Trustees of the British Museum, 1960,0201.2 (h. 8.89 cm)

Figs 16, 17 © The Trustees of the British Museum, 1756,0101.1126

Fig. 18 The sculpture collection of Charles Townley in the entrance hall of his house in Park Street, Westminster (detail) by William Chambers, 1794 © The Trustees of the British Museum 1995,0506.9 (39 x 54 cm)